Cambridge Primary

Computing

Learner's Book 4

Roland Birbal
Carissa Gookool
Michelle Koon Koon
Nazreen Mohammed
Michele Taylor

Series editor:
Roland Birbal

Although every effort has been made to ensure that website addresses are correct at time of going to press, Hodder Education cannot be held responsible for the content of any website mentioned in this book. It is sometimes possible to find a relocated web page by typing in the address of the home page for a website in the URL window of your browser.

Hachette UK's policy is to use papers that are natural, renewable and recyclable products and made from wood grown in well-managed forests and other controlled sources. The logging and manufacturing processes are expected to conform to the environmental regulations of the country of origin.

Orders: please contact Hachette UK Distribution, Hely Hutchinson Centre, Milton Road, Didcot, Oxfordshire, OX11 7HH. Telephone: +44 (0)1235 827827. Email education@hachette.co.uk. Lines are open from 9 a.m. to 5 p.m., Monday to Saturday, with a 24-hour message-answering service. You can also order through our website: www.hoddereducation.com

© Roland Birbal, Carissa Gookool, Michelle Koon Koon, Nazreen Mohammed, Michele Taylor 2022

First published in 2022 by
Hodder Education
An Hachette UK Company
Carmelite House
50 Victoria Embankment
London EC4Y 0DZ

www.hoddereducation.com

Impression number   10 9 8 7 6 5 4 3 2 1
Year   2026 2025 2024 2023 2022

Cover illustration by Lisa Hunt from the Bright Agency
Illustrations by Vian Oelofsen, James Hearne
Typeset in FS Albert 15/17 by IO Publishing CC
Produced by DZS Grafik, Printed in Bosnia & Herzegovina

A catalogue record for this title is available from the British Library.
ISBN 9781398368590

Contents

How to use this book

Get started! Talk about the new topic with a partner or small group.

Get started!

Have you ever played a computer game that seemed to repeat the same thing over and over again?

In small groups, discuss how repetition can be used in the following two types of games:

Sports games

Puzzle games

1 Which parts of these games are repeated?
2 Do the repeated actions make the games fun?
3 How do these games keep you interested in playing?

You will learn:

* about algorithms
* to develop algorithms with repetition
* to test different parts of a program.

In this unit, you will use sub-routines and repetition to create algorithms and computer games in Scratch.

You will learn: A list of things you will learn in the unit.

Warm up

Work with a partner.
1 What is the difference between hardware and software?
2 State which of these objects shown below are hardware and which are software:

Monitor

Chrome™ browser

Mouse

Windows

Scratch

Printer

Keyboard

Webcam

Warm up: An offline activity to start your learning.

Do you remember?

Before starting this unit, check that you:
* can break a task into smaller parts
* can plan a program
* know about loops.

In this unit, you will use Scratch. There is an online chapter all about Scratch.

Do you remember? A list of things you should know before you start the unit.

Learn

Computer programs can contain sub-routines.

A sub-routine is a subset of code within a program. It contains instructions that are used more than once in the program.

For example, in a computer game, there are certain actions that a player repeats throughout the game. Each action uses a sub-routine.

> **Keyword**
> **sub-routine:** a set of instructions designed to perform a frequently-used operation

Algorithm that uses a sub-routine

Look at the algorithms in tables 1 to 5 for the **Dot** sprite in a Chasing Game. In these algorithms, the **Dot** character should do the following:

- Move up when the up arrow is pressed.
- Move down when the down arrow is pressed.
- Move to the left when the left arrow is pressed.
- Move to the right when the right arrow is pressed.

When any of the four arrow keys are pressed, **Dot** should also turn 30 degrees to the right, change costume and bark.

Table 1

Step	Instruction
①	Start program when up arrow key is pressed
②	Change y position by 10
③	Run "Move Around" sub-routine

Tables 1 to 4 show the instructions when each arrow key is pressed. What do you see in the third step in Tables 1 to 4?

Table 2

Step	Instruction
①	Start program when down arrow key is pressed
②	Change y position by –10
③	Run "Move Around" sub-routine

Before creating a computer program with a sub-routine, we can write the algorithm that uses this sub-routine.

Learn: Learn new computing skills with your teacher. Look at the instructions to help you.

Practise: Answer questions to learn more and practise your new skills.

Practise

1 What is each robot doing? Match each letter below to the number of the picture that represents the robot's action.

A This robot is sorting food.

B This robot is delivering packages on the ground.

C This robot is driving a car while the passenger is reading.

D This robot is preparing a hot drink.

E This robot is delivering packages by air.

F This robot is packing boxes that have been sold on a website.

(1)

(2)

(4)

(3)

(5)

(6)

2 State whether the following statements are true or false:

a A self-driving car is also called an AV.

b It is too dangerous to use robots for brain surgery.

c A bus always needs a human driver.

d Packages can only be delivered using robot drones.

e Robots preparing food must look like humans.

Go further:
Activities to make you think carefully about computing.

Go further

1 Look at the algorithm below for a character in a computer game.

Monkey: Part 1

Step	Instruction
1	Start program when space key is pressed
2	Switch to the next costume
3	Run "Jump" sub-routine
4	Say "He-he-he" for 1 second

Monkey: Part 2

Step	Instruction
1	Start "Jump" sub-routine
2	Change y position by 40
3	Wait for 0.2 seconds
4	Change y position by −40

Write, in your own words, what the algorithm does.

Computational thinking

Change the algorithm above to repeat the sub-routine action five times.

Look at the code below created for this game.

2 Create this program in Scratch using the **Monkey** sprite and the **Jungle** Backdrop.

```
define Jump

change y by 40
wait 0.2 seconds
change x by -40
```

```
when space ▼ key pressed
next backdrop
Jump
say Hello! for 2 seconds
```

3 Run your program. Does the program match the algorithm above?
4 Test different parts of the program to identify and debug any errors.

Challenge yourself!

Use the data table below to answer the questions that follow.

Pizza Order	Size	Cost	Name of Customer	Address	Delivery Time
Cheese	Large	$70.00	Hana Jones	10B Abbey Street	6:00 p.m.
Hawaiian	Medium	$60.00	Sadah Remy	12A Dawson Street	4:00 p.m.
Hawaiian	Large	$90.00	Ken George	101 Park Avenue	4:15 p.m.

1 a Write the names of the fields in your notebook.
  b For each field, state the data type.

Remember, the data types are: numbers, text, currency, date/time, yes/no.

  c How many records are in the data table?
2 Perform searches to answer these questions:
  a How many people ordered the Hawaiian pizza?
  b Who ordered a large pizza?
3 Which fields did you look at to answer question **2b**?

Challenge yourself!
A harder activity to test your new skills.

All links to additional resources can be found at: https://www.hoddereducation.co.uk/cambridgeextras

My project

Create a computer drawing game. When you press the space key, one sprite should draw circles in different colours. When you click on another sprite, it should make five stamps of itself.

1 Create a new project and add the **Pen** extension blocks to the palette.
2 Add the **Beetle** sprite and the code below.
3 Run and test your program.
4 Write the algorithm for this character that matches the code.

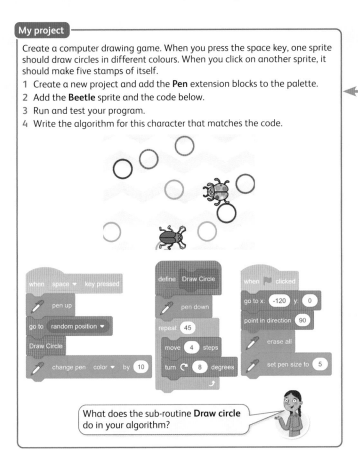

What does the sub-routine **Draw circle** do in your algorithm?

My project:
A longer activity at the end of the unit to test the skills you have learnt so far.

Did you know?

Unpiloted passenger planes are in development. But all modern aircraft already have an autopilot system that allows the plane to fly itself, without help from humans.

Did you know? Learn about interesting facts and information.

What can you do?

Read and review what you can do.
✔ I know about algorithms with a sub-routine.
✔ I can develop algorithms and programs with repetition.
✔ I can systematically test programs.

Great! Now you know sub-routines and can systematically test programs.

What can you do? Find out how much you have learnt and what you can do.

Keyword
sub-routine: a set of instructions designed to perform a frequently-used operation

Keywords: Understand new computing words. The **Glossary** at the end of the book also lists all of these words.

Computational thinking
Change the algorithm above to repeat the sub-routine action five times.

Computational thinking: A task that tests your computational thinking skills.

Creating animations

Get started!

Have you ever seen shows and movies where the characters repeat some actions over and over? In small groups, discuss what actions the following animals could repeat in a movie:

ⓐ lion

ⓑ butterfly

ⓒ snake

ⓓ rabbit

You will learn:

- to follow, understand and correct algorithms with repetition
- to add comments to blocks of code
- to develop programs with repetition.

In this unit, you will create animations using repetition in Scratch.

Warm up

Work in pairs. Look at the sequence of the following dance moves:

①
side step

②
side step

③
spin

④
side step

⑤
side step

⑥
spin

⑦
side step

⑧ ?

Discuss the dance move steps with your partner.

1 How many moves are there in total?

2 Did you notice a pattern in the moves?

3 Which moves were repeated?

4 What do you think is the next move?

Side step and **spin** are two dance moves.

Do you remember?

In this unit, you will use Scratch.

There is an online chapter all about Scratch.

Before starting this unit, check that you:

- know what an algorithm is
- can follow, understand and correct algorithms
- can create programs with more than one algorithm
- can make a change to a block of code.

Understanding loops
Forever loop

Learn

In simple animations, a series of images are repeated. These can make it look like the character is moving.

For instance, repetition is used in an animation of a bird flapping its wings.

Loops are used in programs to repeat instructions.

One type of loop is called a forever loop.

A forever loop is where the instructions repeat forever. The instructions repeat over and over without stopping.

In this unit, we will use a forever loop to have characters repeat actions.

Change an algorithm to perform an action forever

Look at this algorithm for a butterfly. The butterfly glides for 1 second to a random position. In this algorithm, the butterfly only glides once.

Step	Instruction
①	Start program when Green Flag is clicked
②	Set butterfly's position to: x = −168, y = 5
③	Glide 1 second to a random position
④	Stop program

Remember, **x** is horizontal (left–right ⟷) and **y** is vertical (up–down ↕).

Keywords
repetition: code that is run a number of times within a program
forever loop: instructions that repeat over and over without stopping
random: does not follow a pattern

The algorithm can be changed so that it repeats without stopping. We can do this using a forever loop as shown in step 4 below.

Step	Instruction
①	Start program when Green Flag is clicked
②	Set butterfly's position to: x = −168, y = 5
③	Glide 1 second to a random position
④	Repeat step 3 forever
⑤	Stop program

Practise

The algorithm below makes the butterfly flap its wings once. It changes the first image of the butterfly with its wings up to the second image of the butterfly with its wings down.

Step	Instruction
❶	Start program when Green Flag is clicked
❷	Show image of butterfly with its wings up for 0.5 seconds
❸	Show image of butterfly with its wings down for 0.5 seconds

We want to change this algorithm so the butterfly will flap its wings over and over without stopping.

Copy and complete the steps below using a forever loop.

Hint: You want to see both images repeated.

Step	Instruction
❶	Start program when Green Flag is clicked
❷	Show image of butterfly with its wings _____ for 0.5 seconds
❸	Show image of butterfly with its wings _____ for 0.5 seconds
❹	Repeat steps ___ and ___ _____
❺	Stop program

Adding comments

Comments are lines of text added to a program. They are used to explain what the code does. They can help other people understand what the code does. Comments can help with debugging or improving the code in the future. Unlike the rest of the code, comments do not run when a program is started.

In Scratch, we can add comments to any block of code.

Adding a comment to a block of code

Here is the code in Scratch for the butterfly algorithm from page 10. The butterfly glides for 1 second to a random position.

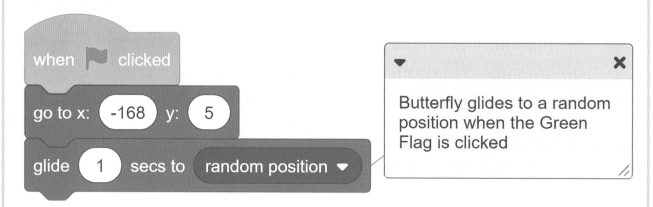

Butterfly glides to a random position when the Green Flag is clicked

To add a comment:

1 Right-click on the block that you want to add a comment to.
2 Select **Add Comment**. A blank yellow box appears.
3 Type the comment in the yellow box.

> **Keywords**
> **comment:** a note explaining the meaning of a program's code
> **debugging:** finding and removing errors from a program

Practise

We will create a program in Scratch with comments. The program will make the butterfly glide once and flap its wings four times.

1 Search for and select the **Butterfly2** sprite.

2 Search for and select the **Blue Sky** Backdrop.

3 Under the **Events** group of blocks, select the **When Green Flag clicked** block.

4 Under the **Looks** group, select the **Switch Costume To** block. From the dropdown arrow, select the **Butterfly2-a** image. In this image, the wings are down.

5 Under the **Control** group of blocks, select the **Wait 1 Seconds** block. Change the **1** second to **0.5** seconds so that each image is shown for half a second.

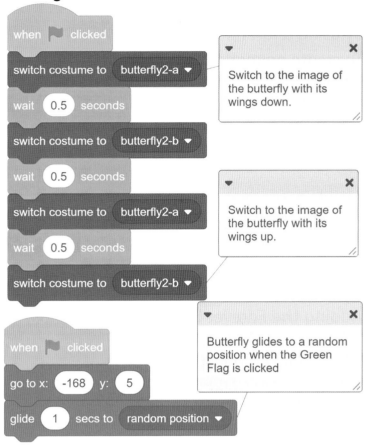

Switch to the image of the butterfly with its wings down.

Switch to the image of the butterfly with its wings up.

Butterfly glides to a random position when the Green Flag is clicked

6 Add the remaining blocks of code as shown.

7 Add comments as shown by following the instructions on page 12.

Try your code. When the **Green Flag** is clicked, the butterfly flaps its wings four times. Then it glides for 1 second to a random position once.

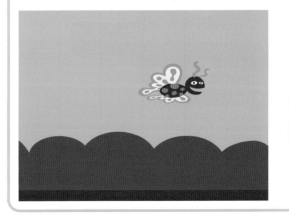

For the butterfly to flap its wings, use the **Switch Costume To** block to switch the images.

Using repetition

Learn

Repetition can be added to a program by using a forever loop.

To create animations with repetition, we use the Forever block. This is found under the **Control** group of blocks.

All the code inside this block will repeat until you stop the program.

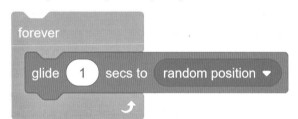

Keyword

Forever block: repeats the code inside it over and over until you stop the program

Instead of adding more of the same blocks of code, we can use the **Forever** block to repeat the same action forever!

Adding the Forever block to a block of code

The **Forever** block can make the butterfly flap its wings up and down over and over. In the left block of code, the butterfly switches costumes four times.

In the right block of code, a **Forever** block is added. The butterfly switches costumes forever until the program is stopped.

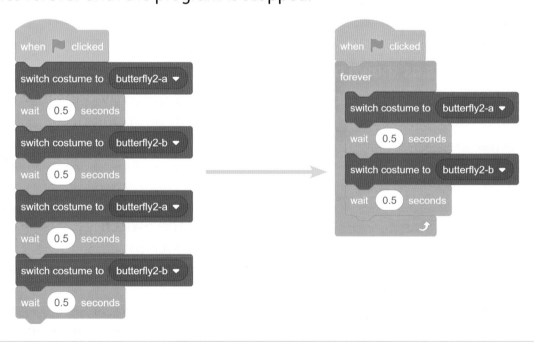

Practise

Open your previous program with the **Butterfly2** sprite.

Add two **Forever** blocks as shown below. This makes the **Butterfly2** sprite flap its wings and glide for 1 second to random positions forever.

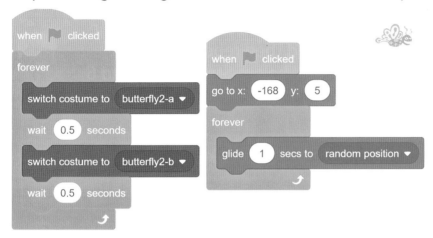

2 Search and select the **Chick** sprite.

3 Place the **Chick** at the left of the screen.

Add the code shown below. You will need to:

i)   use the **Next Costume** block from the **Looks** group

ii) use the **Move 20 Steps** block from the **Motion** group

iii) add **Wait** and **Forever** blocks to each section of code.

> To switch between more than two costumes, you can use the **Next Costume** block.

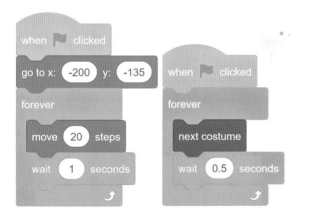

The **Chick** should move forward and change costume forever.

Click the **Green Flag** to run your program.

Discuss with a partner what would happen if you removed the **Wait** block.

Go further

Ava is performing in her school's concert. Create a dance animation for Ava's routine as follows.

Computational thinking

1 Create an algorithm for a ballerina to move 30 steps to the right, then 30 steps to the left, and then repeat forever. Work in pairs to complete the steps below. Steps 1, 2, 4 and 6 have been done for you.

Step	Instruction
1	Start program when Green Flag is clicked
2	Set start position to: x = –66, y = –57
3	
4	Wait 1 second
5	
6	Wait 1 second
7	

2 Create the program for the ballerina using the algorithm. Use the **Ballerina** sprite and **Theater 2** Backdrop.

Hint: To move left, use a negative number in the **Move Steps** block.

3 Add the **Next Costume** block for the ballerina to switch costumes repeatedly.

4 Add comments to the program.

5 Run your program. Check that it looks like the images below.

Challenge yourself!

Make changes to your dance animation from page 16.

1. Add the **Anina Dance** sprite.

2. Change your Backdrop from **Theater 2** to **Spotlight**.

3. Set the starting position of the **Ballerina** sprite to:
   x = –85, y = –61

4. Set the starting position of the **Anina Dance** sprite to:
   x = 94, y = –44

5. Add code to the **Anina Dance** sprite to:
   i)   move 30 steps right, then wait 1 second
   ii) move 30 steps left, then wait 1 second
   iii) repeat steps i) and ii) forever.

6. Program the **Anina Dance** sprite to switch costumes after she moves left.

7. Add the **Start sound** block from the **Sound** group to the **Anina Dance** sprite. Add it before the **Forever** block.

   Try your code. Check that you have completed all tasks.

Hint: The **Anina Dance** sprite has a sound called **Dance Magic**.

Compare the blocks of code for the **Ballerina** and **Anina Dance** sprites.

How are they the same and how are they different? Talk with your partner.

My project

Create your own animated movie with an underwater theme and give it a name, for example: Shark Attack.

1 Copy and complete the table below. Create an algorithm for one of your characters to switch costumes repeatedly. (For example, a **Shark** can open and close its mouth repeatedly.) Think of the instructions for your character.

Step	Instruction
❶	Start program when Green Flag is clicked
❷	Set start position to:
❸	
❹	
❺	

Check the images below for ideas.

2 Choose a sprite and an **Underwater** Backdrop.
3 Add code to move your sprite around repeatedly.
4 Add code to make your sprite switch costumes repeatedly.
5 Add three other sprites of your choice and animate them.
6 Add comments to explain your program.
7 Run your code. Check that you have completed all tasks.

Compare your final program to your partner's program. Is it easy to understand your code and your partner's code?

Did you know?

There are loops all around us, even in nature.
For example:

- The sun rises and sets every day.
- The week begins on a Sunday and ends on a Saturday 52 times in a year.
- Spring, Summer, Autumn and Winter occur every year.

What can you do?

Read and review what you can do.

- ✔ I can follow, understand and correct algorithms with repetition.
- ✔ I can add comments to blocks of code.
- ✔ I can develop programs using the Forever block.

Well done! Now you can create animations with repetition.

Databases

Get started!

Discuss with a partner. Use the pictures to help you with the answers.

- This teacher collects some information from her students.
- She writes each student's information on a sheet of paper.
- She stores each student's information in a file.
- She then places the file in a filing cabinet like this.

Answer 'Yes' or 'No' to these questions.

1 Will the teacher take some time to search for a student file?

2 Can the teacher misplace a file?

3 Will it be difficult to make changes to students' information on paper?

4 Will the teacher need a lot of space to store the files?

Is there a better way for the teacher to store the students' information?

What can she do?

You will learn:

- about paper-based and digital databases
- about using a form to collect data
- about data and information
- to sort data into order.

In this unit, you will learn about databases, forms and sorting data.

Warm up

Work in pairs for this activity. One student will use a search engine on the computer. The other student will use a paper-based dictionary.

Search for these words. Write their meanings in your notebook.

- Data
- Information

Which student was able to find the meanings of the words faster?

Do you think you can find more words using the paper-based dictionary or search engine?

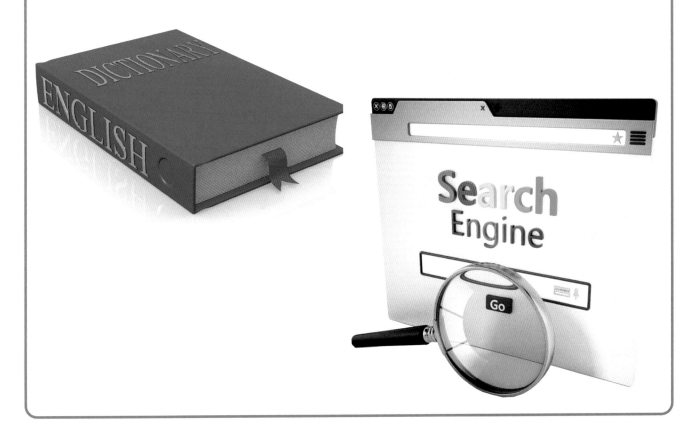

Do you remember?

Before you start this unit, check that you:
- know that a computer can sort and organise data
- know that a computing device can record data using a form
- know that spreadsheets have rows, columns and cells.

Databases
Physical vs Digital databases

A database is a collection of related data. Databases can be physical or digital. Physical databases are paper-based and digital databases are electronic.

Physical databases

Physical databases were the main method of storing data before computers became popular. The data was stored in filing cabinets.

Physical databases are still used by many small organisations.

Some common examples of physical databases are telephone directories, a diary and a printed address book.

Digital databases

A digital database can only be accessed by using a computer.

The picture below shows a computerised sales terminal.
This is a type of digital database.

Keyword
database:
an organised collection of related data

Other businesses that use digital databases are:

- restaurants, for keeping track of food orders
- hospitals, for patient record keeping.

Differences between physical and digital databases	
Physical database	**Digital database**
Data is recorded on paper.	Data is recorded using a computing device.
A lot of space is needed to store data. Data is often stored in big filing cabinets.	Very little storage space is needed. Data is stored on small computer storage devices.
Searching for data can be difficult.	Data is easy to find.
Making changes to data can be hard.	Data is easy to change.
Sorting data is difficult and time-consuming.	Data can be sorted easily and quickly.
Copying data is time-consuming.	Copies of data can be made easily and quickly.

Did you know?

A **manual database** is the same as a physical database.

Practise

1   Copy and complete the sentence using these words:
    organised, **related**, **database**

    A _____ is an _____ collection of

    _____ data.

2   State the type of database shown in each picture: Physical or Digital.

a _____   b _____

3   Copy this table in your notebook. State whether each description is for a physical or digital database.

Description	Physical or Digital
Easy and quick to sort data	
Changes made to the data can be messy	
Data is recorded on paper	
Can easily make a copy of data	
Data can be easily found	
Searching for data can be difficult	

Using forms to collect data
Advantages and disadvantages

A form is a document with headings and spaces to collect data.

Forms can be paper-based or electronic.

Advantages of forms

- Everyone fills in the form in the same way. This makes it easy to compare answers.
- A form can have different types of questions such as Checkboxes and Multiple-choice for easy completion.
  This reduces the amount of writing.
- It is easy to make a copy of a form.
- Forms can be easily sent to lots of people to collect data.
- A form can gather the correct type of data.
- It is a fast way of collecting data.

Disadvantages of forms

- It takes time to design a good form.
- Questions have to be written very carefully. If they are not, it can mean getting the wrong data.
- It costs money to copy paper-based forms.
- People must have a device to complete electronic forms.
- Forms can contain private data. Care must be taken to make sure the wrong people cannot access the form.
- If paper-based forms are destroyed, the data may be lost.

Practise

1 State whether the following statements are true or false:
   a Forms are only paper-based.
   b More writing is required with forms.
   c It takes time to write questions in a form.
   d You must have access to a device to complete an electronic form.

2 David is helping Raj to create a form to collect some data from the members of his cricket team.
   From the statements below, select the advantages of Raj using a form to collect the data from his teammates.

   A It costs money to make copies of a paper-based form.
   B Raj can easily send the forms to his teammates.
   C Raj needs to take time to design the form.
   D Using a form is a fast way to collect data.

3 State whether the following sentences are advantages or disadvantages of using a form to collect data:
   a A poorly-designed form can affect the collection of data.
   b Different people fill out a form in the same way.
   c Almost anyone can fill in a form.
   d If paper-based forms are destroyed, then the data is lost.

4 Can you think of any other advantages and disadvantages of using forms to collect data, besides the ones stated in the **Learn** panel on page 25? Discuss with a partner.

Data vs Information
What is the difference?

Learn

Data can be in the form of numbers, letters, symbols, images and sounds.

Data on its own has no meaning or context. It is unorganised. This raw data needs to be processed to produce information.

For example, if the heights of students in a class are processed by a computer, we can get information such as:

- the tallest student in class
- the shortest student in class
- the average height of the students in the class.

Information is useful because it is organised and has some context and meaning.

Other examples of data and information are shown below.

Data	Information
Cost of items	The most expensive item
Marks of students	The student who scored the lowest mark in the test
Daily temperature	The coldest day in the month of January

Keywords

raw data: not processed
information: processed data

The first table below shows raw data. We do not know what the numbers mean.

5	18
5	17
7	15
10	11
13	8
16	5

The second table shows the average monthly temperature in London. Now we know what the numbers mean. This is an example of information.

Month	Temperature in °C	Month	Temperature in °C
January	5	July	18
February	5	August	17
March	7	September	15
April	10	October	11
May	13	November	8
June	16	December	5

Practise

1 State which of the following is data and which is information:
   a The weight of each student in class.
   b The average rainfall for the month of July.
   c The flavour of ice-cream each person chose at the ice-cream parlour.
   d The least favourite flavour ice-cream.
   e The most popular sport at school.

Choose the correct answer in each case.

2 Raw data is _____.
   a processed
   b unprocessed
   c organised

3 Information is _____ data.
   a processed
   b unprocessed
   c raw

4 Data is _____.
   a meaningful
   b meaningless

5 Information is _____.
   a useless
   b useful

6 Data is _____.
   a organised letters and numbers
   b unorganised letters and numbers

7 Information is _____.
   a organised letters and numbers
   b unorganised letters and numbers

Sorting data
Ascending and descending order

Learn

Data can be sorted using a spreadsheet. The **Sort** feature is used to put data in ascending or descending order.

Ascending order – all the names in the blue column are organised in the order of A to Z.

If two names have the same first letter, then the second letters of the names are compared to see which comes first.

The name 'Amy' appears before 'Annay' because 'm' is before 'n' in the alphabet.

Descending order – all the names in the green column are organised in the order of Z to A.

In this case, the name 'Annay' appears before 'Amy' because the list is sorted in descending order.

Numbers can be sorted from the smallest to largest number, or the largest to smallest number.

The blue column shows a list of people sorted in ascending order by Age.

The green column shows a list of people sorted in descending order by Age.

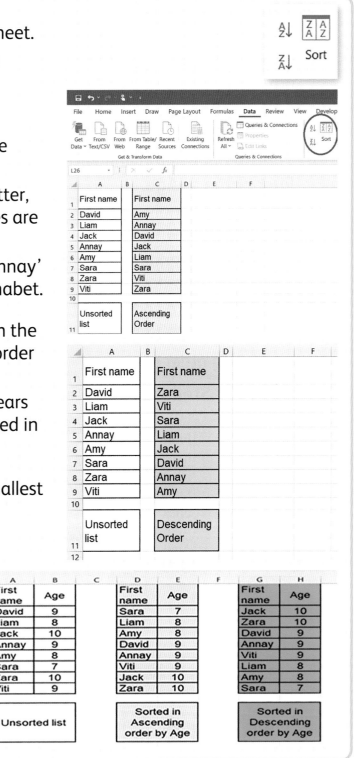

Practise

1 To practise the various 'Sorts' in the **Learn** panel on page 29, you will need a computer and spreadsheet software. Your teacher will help with this activity.

a Type the list as seen in step 1 below.

b Click on all the cells, including the headings (**First name** and **Age**). The data becomes highlighted in grey.

c Click on the **Data** tab.

d Click on the **Sort** command.

e Choose the column you wish to sort by, using the drop-down options: **First name** or **Age**.

f To sort in ascending order, click on **A to Z** or **Smallest to Largest** in the **Order** drop-down menu.

g To sort in descending order, click on **Z to A** or **Largest to Smallest** in the **Order** drop-down menu.

2 Follow the steps to sort the list in:

a ascending order by **First name**.
b descending order by **First name**.
c ascending order by **Age**.
d descending order by **Age**.

Step 1   **Step 2**   **Step 3**

Step 4   **Step 5**

3 Karim typed these items in a spreadsheet. Write the items to show how they would be sorted in ascending order.

pencil   ruler   notebook   markers   paper

Go further

1 Which of these statements describes a digital database?

   a A lot of physical storage space is needed.

   b Changes to the data can be made easily.

   c Searching for data can be difficult.

   d Copies of data can be made quickly.

2 Identify the statements that describe a disadvantage of using a form when collecting data.

   a Less writing.

   b Must have a device for electronic forms.

   c There is a cost attached to making copies of paper-based forms.

   d Can easily distribute a form to multiple persons.

3 Draw these boxes in your notebook.

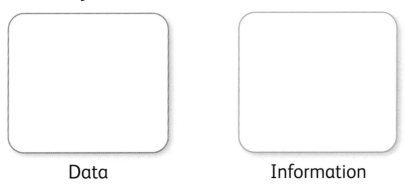

          Data   Information

Write the correct words in the boxes that describe data and information.

(raw) (meaningless) (organised) (processed) (no context) (meaningful)

4 a Write these words in ascending order.

    (dolphin) (dinosaur) (fish) (crab)

   b Write these same words in descending order.

5 a Write these numbers in ascending order.

    (12) (20) (35) (5) (47)

   b Write these same numbers in descending order.

Challenge yourself!

Work in pairs.

1 a State two differences between data and information.

   b Give one example of data and one example of information.

2 Ravi has a computer but Suri does not. Who will be able to complete an electronic form?

3 Give one advantage and one disadvantage of using a form to collect data.

4 You will need a computer and spreadsheet to complete this activity.

   a Type the names of five of your friends or family members in the spreadsheet (in Column A).

   b Sort the names in ascending order and descending order.

   c Type their ages in the column next to their names (in Column B).

   d Sort the list of ages in ascending order and descending order.

Do you remember that the **Sort** feature is used to sort the data in the spreadsheet?

My project

Work in pairs to create your own physical database.

1 Get five index cards. Write the headings on each card as seen in Example A below. Write data about five different people on each separate index card, as seen in Example B.

   a How can we sort the cards?

   b What will you do if data needs to be changed on an index card?

   c What will you do if you have to get a sixth person's information?

A ABOUT ME	B ABOUT ME
Name:	Name: Jane Doe ....
Age:	Age: 8 years ....
Birthday month:	Birthday month: June ....

2 Sort the index cards in ascending order by **Birthday Month**. Write the order on a sheet of paper.

3 Sort the cards in descending order by **Age**. Write the order on a sheet of paper.

4 Type the data from the index cards in a spreadsheet, using the headings shown in the example on the right.

- Sort the list by **Birthday Month** in ascending order.
- Sort the list by **Age** in descending order.

5 Discuss the following with your partner:

- Which sort was faster – sorting the index cards or sorting the list on the spreadsheet?
- Would you consider using an electronic form to gather this data?
- What is ONE disadvantage of using an electronic form to collect the data?
- What information could be produced from this data?

What can you do?

Read and review what you can do.

- ✔ I know about paper-based and digital databases.
- ✔ I understand the advantages and disadvantages of using a form.
- ✔ I know the differences between data and information.
- ✔ I can sort data into order.

Great work! Now you know about databases, using forms and sorting data!

Wired and wireless networks

Get started!

Discuss with your partner.

1 What type of network is in your school or home – is it a wired or wireless network? Could it be both?

2 Which devices form part of the network?

3 What are some of the services available on the network?

4 Does the network allow digital files to be shared?

5 Does the network allow access to the World Wide Web?

6 Do computers on the network have access to all the resources on the network?

7 What are some of the advantages and disadvantages of a network?

In this unit, you will learn more about wired and wireless networks.

You will learn:

- about servers and clients
- about the difference between the World Wide Web and the internet
- about the differences between Wi-Fi® and ethernet.

Warm up

Work in groups. Pretend you are in a restaurant. Draw pictures of items on the menu on separate pieces of paper – meals, drinks and desserts.

One student will be the waiter. The other students will be the customers.

Customers should individually order meals, drinks and desserts from the waiter.

The waiter should write each order, find the correct pictures and then provide a picture of each requested item to each customer, if available.

Discuss the following questions in your groups:

1 What is the role of a customer?

2 What is the role of the waiter?

3 Does each customer have equal access to the waiter?

4 How can customers get faster service? For example, is it possible to have different waiters for each type of item?

Do you remember?

Before you start this unit, check that you:

• know about wired and wireless networks

• know about hardware on a network

• know about things you can do on a network.

Servers and clients

A network consists of two types of computers: servers and clients.

Servers

A server stores, finds and sends files and data to other computers on its network.

A server also allows other computers to share resources and communicate with one another.

Keywords

server: a computer that provides services to other computers on a network

client: a computer that connects to and uses the resources of a server

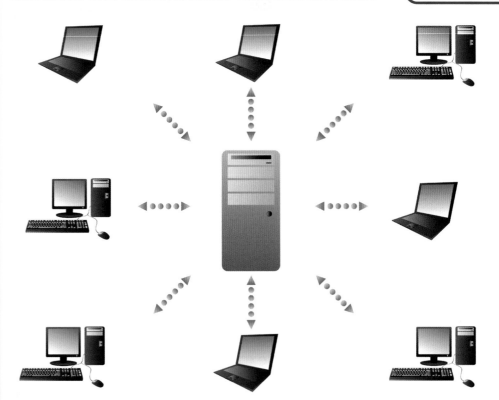

Servers can do many different things. Some networks may have more than one server for different roles. Here are some typical servers:

- **File servers** store files for everyone on the network.
- **Application servers** allow programs to be run over a networks.
- **Web servers** hold and share web pages.
- **Print servers** forward documents from clients to be printed.
- **Mail servers** handle emails between users.

Clients

A client is a computer that requests services from the server.

The server checks each request and then sends the response.

Client–server networks

Client–server networks are used in schools and businesses where many computers need access to the same information or devices.

For example:

- In a school, a teacher using a client computer connected to the network can request information about a student from the file server.

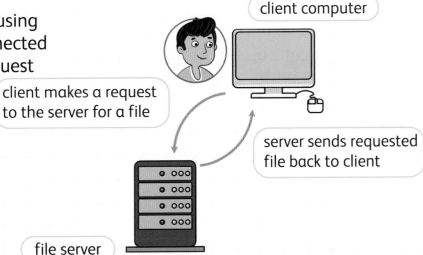

client computer

client makes a request to the server for a file

server sends requested file back to client

file server

- Teachers in different classrooms in a school can send documents to a printer in the office. The teacher's computer sends a request to the print server. The print server receives the request and provides the teacher with access to the printer. The printer then prints the document.

- Similarly, if you want to access a file on the internet, you use a browser to send a request to a web server. The web server accepts the request, finds the requested document, and sends it back to your browser.

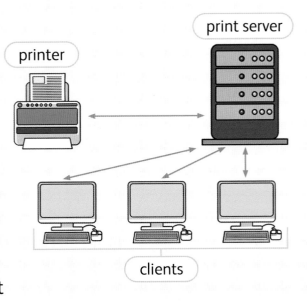

print server

printer

clients

Practise

1 Copy these sentences. Fill in the blank spaces in each sentence with the words provided.

web   communicate   stores   share   requests

a A client computer _____ services from a server.

b A server manages and _____ files, and provides services on a network.

c A _____ server holds and shares web pages.

d A server controls the network and allows clients to _____ resources and _____ with one another.

2 State whether the following statements are true or false:

a A server may be required to service many clients at the same time.

b A typical server may have a faster processing speed than a client computer.

c Servers can only perform one function in a network.

d A print server provides access to the printer when a client makes a request to print a document.

e Schools do not use client–server networks.

3 Name the type of server that will accomplish the following tasks:

a Handle email between users

b Allow programs to run on the network

c Store files in a centralised location so that all users on the network have equal access to the resources.

4 With the aid of a diagram, explain how a client accesses a web page on a client–server network.

Internet and the World Wide Web

Learn

The internet is a worldwide collection of computer networks. It connects millions of computers and other devices.

The internet is made up of many clients and servers.

The clients are devices such as:

- desktops
- smartphones
- laptops.

The servers are the computers that store the information.

Clients request information from the servers, and the servers send it to the clients.

Many people believe that the internet and the World Wide Web are the same thing, but they are not.

The World Wide Web is one of the services offered on the internet.

There are other services on the internet that are not part of the World Wide Web, such as:

- email
- video conferencing
- social network apps
- instant messaging apps.

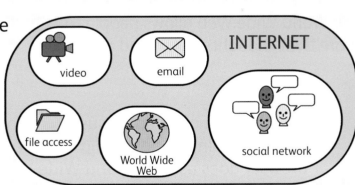

The internet also lets users find and access files stored on computers across the internet.

Do you know of other services offered on the internet?

Keywords

internet: a worldwide network of computers and devices

instant messaging: a service where users can communicate in real time

The World Wide Web (WWW) is a large collection of web pages. These web pages are accessed via the internet using special software called web browsers.

Each web page can be a mix of text, pictures, sounds, video and animations. These pages are linked together using hyperlinks.

Each hyperlink points to another web page. When you click a link, your browser fetches the page from a web server via the internet.

Some of the most popular browsers are: Chrome™ browser, Microsoft Edge and Firefox.

A collection of related web pages is called a website. Every web page has an address so that browsers can find it.

The World Wide Web allows people to share their thoughts, ideas and opinions.

Web server

Web browser requests the web server

Web server serves the web page

Web browser

Chrome™ browser

Firefox

Internet Explorer

Microsoft Edge

Social media apps do not use the World Wide Web. But using social media websites via a browser does use the World Wide Web!

Keywords
World Wide Web: a large collection of linked web pages accessed by a browser
browser: a computer program for displaying and moving between web pages
hyperlink: a link from one web page to another
website: a collection of linked web pages

Did you know?

The World Wide Web was invented by Tim Berners-Lee in 1989. There are currently 4.66 billion active internet users worldwide.

Practise

1 Copy these sentences. Fill in the blank spaces to complete the sentences.
   a The _____ is a worldwide collection of computer networks that connects millions of computers.
   b The World Wide Web is a(n) _____ that runs on the internet.
   c A combination of related web pages is called a _____.
   d Chrome™ browser is an example of a _____.
   e Web pages on the WWW are linked together using _____.

2 State whether the following statements are true or false:
   a The WWW is another name for the internet.
   b The WWW is a service offered on the internet.
   c Browsers are used to find web pages on the internet.
   d Each web page has an address.
   e Video conferencing is a service offered on the internet.
   f The internet utilises web browsers to access information.
   g The WWW is collection of information that can be accessed using the internet.
   h A social network app is a service on the WWW.
   i A chat room is a place on the internet where users with common interests can communicate.

3 List two services available on the internet.

4 State two differences between the World Wide Web and the internet.

Wi-Fi and ethernet

Learn

Networks can be classified as wired or wireless.

Ethernet is a name given to copper cables that connect computers in a wired network. It lets devices communicate with one another.

Wired networks are used for devices that are unlikely to move. This is because the cables limit the ability to move away from the connection.

An ethernet network is usually more reliable with higher speeds and more secure than a wireless network.

Wireless networks use invisible radio wave signals to connect devices, so they can share information and resources.

To communicate over wireless networks, computers and other devices use a set of rules known as Wi-Fi. Devices connected using Wi-Fi can be easily moved around.

Wireless networks:

- have a shorter range – up to 50 metres

- are slower than wired networks

- are easier to steal information from.

Wireless networks are popular in homes and schools; anywhere where devices are often added or removed.

	Wired networks using ethernet	**Wireless networks using Wi-Fi**
Installation	Difficult to set up	Easier to install
Speed	Faster data transfer speeds	Slower data transfer speeds
Reliability	More reliable – deliver a consistent data transfer speed	Less reliable – Wi-Fi signals can be lost
Mobility	Devices cannot move as they have to be connected to a wire	Devices can move wherever the Wi-Fi signal is available
Security	More secure than a wireless network	Less secure – may be more vulnerable to viruses and hacking
Common devices	Desktops, servers	Laptops, tablets, smartphones, games consoles and security cameras

Keywords

ethernet: another name for the copper cables used in wired networks

wired: connecting devices in a network with physical wires

wireless: a way of connecting devices in a network via radio waves

radio wave: a way of sending information through the air

Wi-Fi: a set of rules for devices communicating over wireless networks

Practise

1 Copy these sentences. Fill in the blank spaces to complete the sentences.

  a A wired network uses _____ to form the connections between the networked devices.

  b Devices in a wired network are _____ mobile than devices in a wireless network.

  c Devices on a wireless network can connect to each other and the internet using _____.

  d The transmission speed over a wireless network is _____ than that of a wired network.

2 True or false?

  a Networks can be classified as wired or wireless.

  b Devices on a wireless network are less mobile than devices on a wired network.

  c Wired networks are more secure than wireless networks.

  d Wireless networks are less vulnerable to hackers than wired networks.

  e Wireless networks are popular in homes.

3 Select the most appropriate answer.

  a Wired networks are most popular in _____.

  (homes) (offices)

  b Wired networks have _____ mobility.

  (lower) (higher)

Go further

1 State whether the following statements are true or false:
   a Web servers allow programs to be run over a network.
   b One of the functions of the server is to evaluate each request for resources from a client and to respond.
   c A server allows client computers on a network to communicate with one another.
   d Devices can only connect to the internet when connected to a network with a wire.
   e Email is a service offered on the internet.
   f A web page can contain text, pictures, audio and video clips, and animations.
   g Hyperlinks are used to link web pages.
   h Firefox is used to access data from the internet.

2 Match the words to their correct explanations.

Application servers	are computers that form part of the network
Web servers	evaluate each request and then send the response
Client computers	allow programs to be run over a network
Servers	handle emails between users
Mail servers	hold and share web pages

Challenge yourself!

1 A program that allows access to the World Wide Web is called a _____.

2 _____ networks tend to have faster transmission speeds than _____ networks.

3 Give two examples of communication services offered on the internet.

4 Why do some servers have a faster processor, more memory and more storage space than a client computer?

5 Which internet services enable users to locate and use electronic files stored on computers across the internet?

6 Tell your partner what type of network is shown in the picture below.

   a State the names of the different devices shown in this picture.

   b Explain how a page can be printed in this network.

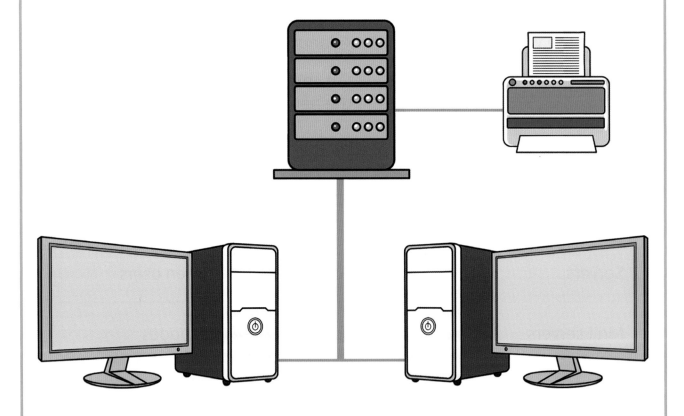

7 What are two limitations of a wireless network?

My project

Nadia learnt about computer networks at school. When she got home, she advised her parents to set up a home computer network. However, they do not understand:

- what a network is
- the advantages and disadvantages of setting up a home network
- the role of clients and servers
- the differences between Wi-Fi and ethernet.

Prepare a report to answer the concerns of her parents and these questions below:

1 Which type of network (wired or wireless) would you recommend?

2 Write a short paragraph about the reasons for your choice of network.

3 Draw a sketch of what the computer network might look like.

What can you do?

Read and review what you can do.

- ✔ I know about servers and clients.
- ✔ I can describe the difference between the World Wide Web and the internet.
- ✔ I know about the differences between Wi-Fi and ethernet.

Great job! Now you understand more about networks, the internet and the World Wide Web!

Storytelling

Get started!

With your partner, discuss your favourite songs.
- How many verses does your song have?
- What is the chorus in your song?
- Can you sing your song to your partner?
- Which parts of the song repeat?

In this unit, you will learn to tell stories using iteration and repetition.

You will learn:
- about count-controlled loops
- to use repetition in an algorithm
- to develop a program with the Repeat block.

Warm up

Work in groups. Look at the pictures below. They tell the story of 'Goldilocks and the Three Bears'. Arrange the pictures in the correct order to tell the story.

1 What is the story about?
2 What is repeated in the story?
3 How often is it repeated?

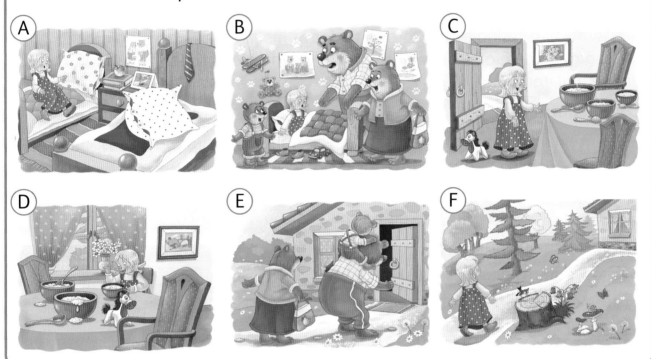

In this unit, you will use Scratch. There is an online chapter all about Scratch.

Do you remember?

Before starting this unit, check that you:
- can follow, understand and correct algorithms with repetition
- know how to develop programs with repetition.

Algorithms
Iteration and count-controlled loops

You have previously learnt that when a series of actions are repeated, it is called a loop. You also learnt that loops are used in programming to repeat a set of instructions.

An iteration is a single pass through a set of instructions within an algorithm or program. Therefore, when a loop is repeated several times, we say that there are several iterations.

Count-controlled loop

A counter can be used to keep track of the number of times a loop occurs. A loop in which a counter is used like this is known as a count-controlled loop. A count-controlled loop is an example of iteration.

These instructions to draw a square can contain a count-controlled loop:

1 Place pen on paper.

2 Draw a 5 cm line.

3 Turn a quarter turn right.

4 Repeat steps 2 and 3 three more times.

5 Remove pen from paper.

In an arcade basketball game, a player is allowed five attempts to shoot a basketball through the hoop.

1 Start the game.

2 Pick up the basketball.

3 Shoot the basketball at the basketball hoop.

4 Award one point if the basketball goes through the hoop.

5 Repeat steps 2, 3 and 4 four more times.

6 End game.

The algorithm will repeat steps 2, 3 and 4 a total of five times. This means that there are five iterations of these steps.

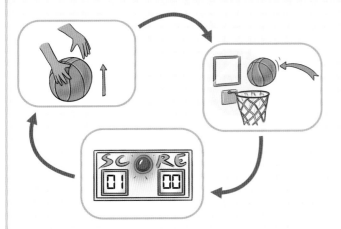

On a racetrack, cars race each other for a number of laps.

This algorithm is for a four-lap race. The following instructions are repeated:

| Drive past the crowd |
| Finish the lap |

These instructions are repeated 4 times.

Algorithm name: Car Race	
Step	**Instruction**
①	Start the race
②	**Drive past the crowd**
③	**Finish the lap**
④	**Drive past the crowd**
⑤	**Finish the lap**
⑥	**Drive past the crowd**
⑦	**Finish the lap**
⑧	**Drive past the crowd**
⑨	**Finish the lap**
⑩	End the race
⑪	Stop car

Did you know?

Iterations occur everywhere. For example, when singing a song, we repeat the chorus several times. This is an example of iteration.

Keywords
iteration: a single pass through a set of instructions
counter: keeps track of the number of times a loop has run
count-controlled loop: a type of loop where instructions are repeated a set number of times

1 State whether the following statements are true or false:
   a When instructions are repeated, it is called a loop.
   b A count-controlled loop tells us how many times a loop is repeated.
   c A set of instructions repeated once is known as an iteration.
   d In a count-controlled loop, you cannot tell how many times an instruction is to be repeated.
   e You cannot have a set of instructions do more than one iteration.

2 You have been asked to fill an empty jug with water using a glass. The algorithm below has been written to perform this task. Once the algorithm is complete, the jug is full of water.

Step	Instruction
1	Start
2	Fill glass with water
3	Pour water from glass into jug
4	Fill glass with water
5	Pour water from glass into jug
6	Fill glass with water
7	Pour water from glass into jug
8	Stop

Answer the following questions:
   a State which instruction or instructions are repeated.
   b Can you state how many times the instructions are repeated? That is, how many iterations of the instructions are needed to fill the jug?
   c What would happen if there were more iterations?
   d What would happen if there were fewer iterations?

Algorithms
Make algorithms shorter

Learn

In a count-controlled loop, you know the exact number of times the loop is repeated. The counter keeps track of how many times a loop runs. The loop ends when the counter reaches a certain number.

Look again at the algorithm **Car Race**. We can shorten it by using a count-controlled loop.

Algorithm name: Car Race	
Step	**Instruction**
①	Start the race
②	Drive past the crowd
③	Finish the lap
④	Drive past the crowd
⑤	Finish the lap
⑥	Drive past the crowd
⑦	Finish the lap
⑧	Drive past the crowd
⑨	Finish the lap
⑩	End the race
⑪	Stop car

Algorithm name: Car Race Shortened	
Step	**Instruction**
①	Start the race
②	Drive past the crowd
③	Finish the lap
④	**Repeat steps 2 and 3, three more times**
⑤	End the race
⑥	Stop car

The longer algorithm has 11 steps and the shorter algorithm has 6 steps.

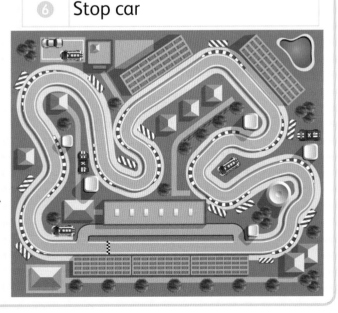

1 State whether the following statements are true or false:

   a A count-controlled loop is when instructions are repeated an unknown number of times.

   b The number of times a loop is executed is called a counter.

   c A counter can keep track of the number of iterations in an algorithm.

   d A loop cannot be repeated.

2 Jack writes the instructions to walk in a square as shown below.
   Help Jack shorten his code by reducing the number of instructions.

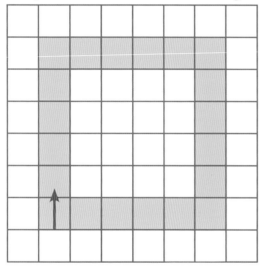

Algorithm name: Square	
Step	**Instruction**
①	Start
②	Move forward 5 blocks
③	Turn right
④	Move forward 5 blocks
⑤	Turn right
⑥	Move forward 5 blocks
⑦	Turn right
⑧	Move forward 5 blocks
⑨	Turn right
⑩	Stop

Algorithm to code
Repeat block in Scratch

Learn

If we know how many times to repeat instructions, we can use a count-controlled loop.

Keyword
Repeat block: Scratch code used for count-controlled loops

The Repeat block allows us to write count-controlled loops in Scratch. It repeats a set of instructions a certain number of times. The counter keeps track of the number of times the instruction is repeated. When we use the **Repeat** block, we do not have to write the same code many times.

For example, if you want to move 10 steps five times, you need to place the **Move 10 steps** block within the **Repeat** block. The **Repeat** block can be found under the **Control** group of blocks.

Look at this example of an algorithm of a tree growing five times and moving 50 steps, and the corresponding Scratch program.

Algorithm name: Grow tree	
Step	**Instruction**
①	Start program when Green Flag is clicked
②	Display tree at 50% size
③	Create copy of tree
④	Grow tree by 10
⑤	Move tree 50 steps
⑥	Repeat steps 3 to 5 four more times
⑦	Stop program

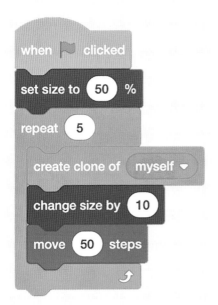

This algorithm can be recreated using Scratch.

Open Scratch and create the program to make a **Tree** sprite grow in size.
In order for your sprite to grow, you have to change its size.

1 Search and select a **Tree** sprite.
2 Under the **Events** group of blocks, select the **When Green Flag clicked** block.
3 Under the **Look** group, select **set size to 100 %**. Change the **100** to **50**.
4 Under the **Control** group of blocks, select the **repeat (10)** block. Change the **10** value to **5**.
5 Under the **Control** group of blocks, select **create clone of (myself)**. This will show a copy of the tree.

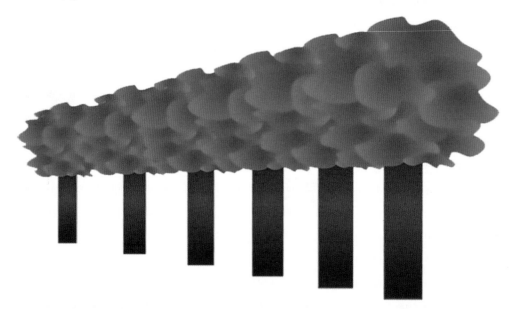

6 Under the **Look** group, select **change size by 10**.
7 Under the **Motions** group, select the **move (10) steps** block. Change the **10** value to **50**.

Note: The repeat instructions in the algorithm come **after** the instructions to be repeated. In the Scratch program, the Repeat block is placed first and **then** the instructions to be repeated are placed within the block.

Practise

Open Scratch and create a program for a sprite to draw a square.
In order to create a square, your sprite has to change directions.
The algorithm for drawing a square is shown below.

Step	Instruction
1	Start program when Green Flag is clicked
2	Put pen down
3	Move forward 100 steps
4	Turn right 90 degrees
5	Move forward 100 steps
6	Turn right 90 degrees
7	Move forward 100 steps
8	Turn right 90 degrees
9	Move forward 100 steps
10	Turn right 90 degrees
11	Stop program

Now follow these instructions to create the program in Scratch.

1 Search and select a suitable sprite and backdrop.
2 Under the **Events** group, select the **When Green Flag clicked** block.
3 Under the **Motions** group, select the **go to x: (0), y: (0)** block. Keep the **x** value as **0** and the **y** value as **0**.
4 Click the **Add Extension** block. Click the **Pen** option.
5 Under the **Pen** group, select the **Pen Down** block.
6 Under the **Control** group of blocks, select the **wait 1 seconds** block so that each image stays in the position for 1 second before turning.

7 Under the **Motion** group, select the **turn (15) degrees clockwise** block and change the **15** degrees to **90**.

8 Under the **Motions** group, select the **Move (10) steps** block and change the **10** steps to **100** steps.

Add blocks to repeat steps 6 to 8 three more times.

Try your code see what happens when the Green Flag is clicked. You should see that your sprite draws a square.

Which steps are repeated?

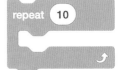

Now edit your code and use the **Repeat** block to reduce the number of steps.

Go further

1 Copy these sentences and fill in the blanks using the words below.

(infinite) (iteration) (count-controlled)

a An _____ is one execution of a loop. There are two types of loops _____ and _____ loops.

b A _____ loop is repeated a fixed number of times.

2 Choose the correct ending for the sentence.
A count-controlled loop _____

a loops an indefinite number of times.

b uses a counter to keep track of the number of times a loop is executed.

c cannot keep track of the number of times a loop is executed.

d is executed an unspecified number of times.

3 Discuss the following question with your partner:

Why do you need to shorten a loop using the repeat command?

4 Your school is having a charity cake sale and wants to show how many cakes have been baked.

a Look at the algorithm on the next page.

b Rewrite the algorithm so that it is shorter.

c Create a Scratch program from your rewritten algorithm using the **Repeat** block.

d If 25 people baked cakes, how would your algorithm change?

Algorithm name: Cake donation	
Step	**Instruction**
①	Start program when Green Flag is clicked
②	Choose a random position on the screen
③	Wait 1 second
④	Display Cake sprite
⑤	Choose a random position on the screen
⑥	Wait 1 second
⑦	Display another Cake sprite
⑧	Choose a random position on the screen
⑨	Wait 1 second
⑩	Display another Cake sprite
⑪	Stop program

Challenge yourself!

David is preparing peanut butter and jelly sandwiches for him and his three sisters. He writes an algorithm to prepare a peanut butter and jelly sandwich:

1
bread slices

2
peanut butter on bread slice

3
jelly on bread slice

4
peanut butter and jelly sandwich

1 Is this a count-controlled loop?
2 How many iterations are there in this algorithm?

Algorithm name: PB&J Sandwich	
Step	Instruction
❶	Start
❷	Cut bread slices
❸	Place peanut butter on one bread slice
❹	Place jelly on one bread slice
❺	Put slices together
❻	Stop

3 How many iterations does David need to make in order for him to prepare the total number of sandwiches he needs?
4 Which steps need to be repeated for David to make the number of sandwiches he needs?
5 Rewrite the algorithm so that it includes the number of iterations to make the correct number of sandwiches.

Computational thinking

David's two brothers also want a sandwich. However, one brother does not like peanut butter and the other brother does not like jelly.

1 Rewrite the algorithm so that David makes all the sandwiches for his sisters and brothers. Compare answers with a partner and discuss any differences.
2 If each of David's siblings wants two sandwiches instead of one, how would you rewrite the algorithm? Share your answer with your partner.

My project

A supermarket worker is putting cartons of milk, loaves of bread, and jars of jelly on a shelf. There are three boxes: one box contains 10 cartons of milk, the second box contains 10 loaves of bread and the third box contains 10 jars of jelly.

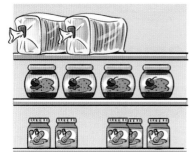

The supermarket worker reaches inside the first box containing the cartons of milk and places each milk carton on the shelf one by one. He repeats this until the box of milk cartons is empty.

He then does the same with the box of bread loaves, until that box is empty. Then he does the same with the box of jelly jars, until that box is empty.

1   Write an algorithm out in full to restock the supermarket shelf with the milk, bread and jelly.

2   Which actions are repeated?

3   State how many times the supermarket worker has to perform each process.

4   Now shorten your algorithm by using the repeat command. Add more rows if you need to.

5   Recreate your algorithm in Scratch. Each time an item is removed from a box you should display it on the screen. You can use the sprites called **Milk**, **Bread** and **Jar**.

Step	Instruction
①	Start
②	
③	
④	
⑤	Stop

Hint: You may need more than one repeat command!

What can you do?

Read and review what you can do.

✔ I can understand algorithms that use count-controlled loops.

✔ I can use repetition to make an algorithm shorter.

✔ I can develop programs using the Repeat block.

Great job! Now you know how to use count-controlled loops and the Repeat block!

Be a computer scientist

Computer scientists and robots

Get started!

Computers have changed most things in our lives. You come into contact with a computer or a computer-controlled device every day.

With a partner, list the ways that you come into contact with a computer or a computer-controlled device on a daily basis. See below for some examples.

Using an electronic toothbrush

Using the bathroom scale

Warming food in the microwave

Attending school online

In this unit, you will learn about the roles of computer scientists and robots.

You will learn:

- about the roles of a computer scientist
- about the roles of robots in deliveries, transport and healthcare.

Warm up

Computer systems are used in many day-to-day objects. They can make certain tasks easier. Some examples are shown below.

Work with a partner. Can you think of two household items that do not use a computer? If a computer system were added, can you think of some things it could do? For example:

• a computer-controlled cup that could keep your drink cool

• a dog's water bowl that could tell you when it is empty and needs refilling.

Do you remember?

Before starting this unit, check that you:

• know the differences between hardware and software

• can name some manual and automatic input devices

• know that computers can control machines

• know about the roles of robots in manufacturing.

The computer scientist
Role in industry

Learn

An important job is that of a computer scientist.

Computer scientists use computational thinking skills to solve problems.

- They might create, design and build products to solve problems.
- They might help to design and build a robot to pack boxes in a factory.
- They might write software for a computer.

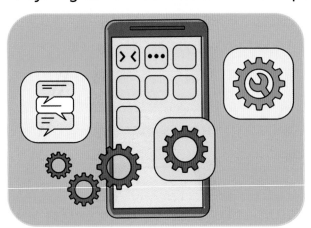

Work in groups. With your group, discuss what software or app you would like a computer scientist to create.

This is Chris. He is a computer hardware engineer.

He designs and tests computer hardware such as the CPU. The CPU and other hardware make up the computer.

He has to understand complicated computer systems in his job.

Computer hardware engineer

Keyword

computer scientist: a person who uses computational thinking skills to work with computer hardware and software

This is Manjit. She is a games developer and programmer.

She writes programs for games played on smartphones and tablets.

She needs to know a lot about programming, and a few different programming languages, in order to create these games.

Games developer and programmer

This is Archer. He is a software developer and he works for a large social media company.

He looks at code for social media apps, and tries to find ways to make it better.

He has to understand a lot about networks in his job.

Software developer

This is Dana. She is a data analyst and works for a chain of supermarkets.

She collects and organises data. She uses the data to ask questions, make decisions and find answers. She looks at data about shopping habits to find out what people buy.

A data analyst explains what she finds to people with little knowledge of computing.

Data analyst

This is Danny. He is a robotics engineer.

He works in the space industry, and designs and builds robots.

He works with other computer scientists, such as programmers who write programs to tell the robot what to do.

Robotics engineer

As you can see, a computer scientist can have many different roles. But in almost all roles, a computer scientist:

- looks at problems and decides how they can be solved
- breaks down problems into smaller, less complicated problems that are easier to solve
- works as part of a team with people who do not know very much about computing – this might include graphic artists, business specialists, salespeople and accountants.

This computer scientist is building a computer part.

Practise

1 Which one of these statements is **not** true about computer scientists?

  a A computer scientist can improve the performance of computer systems.

  b A computer scientist does not work as part of a team to do research.

  c A computer scientist creates solutions to solve problems.

  d A computer scientist can help to design and build new computer hardware.

2 State whether the following statements are true or false:

  a Game developers and programmers are not computer scientists.

  b Social media companies hire computer scientists to improve the code in social media apps.

  c A person who designs computer chips and computer parts is a computer scientist.

  d A robotics engineer is a computer scientist who works alone to build robots.

  e A data analyst is a type of computer scientist whose job is to retrieve, collect and organise data and information.

3 Work in groups.

  a A computer scientist job has become available. You have been asked to create a flyer to advertise the post. Draw some images of the different roles a computer scientist might undertake.

  Include in your flyer some of the general skills that a computer scientist would be expected to have.

  b Research three more industries that have not been covered in this section. What roles might a computer scientist have in each industry?

Robots in service industries

Robots are used in many industries to perform different tasks. They are used in the transport, food and healthcare industries, and many others.

Delivery

Robots are used to deliver items.

For example, some companies use flying robots called drones to deliver packages.

Some restaurants use delivery robots to deliver food to customers.

Transportation

Another type of robot is a driverless vehicle.

Self-driving cars are not driven by people. These cars use several different sensors to move from one place to the next without causing an accident.

Self-driving cars are also known as driverless cars, robo-cars, autonomous vehicles or AVs.

There are also driverless buses and driverless trains.

Did you know?

Unpiloted passenger planes are in development. But all modern aircraft already have an autopilot system that allows the plane to fly itself, without help from humans.

Keywords

drone: a remote-controlled, unmanned or pilotless aircraft

sensor: a device that detects an input from the environment, such as heat, light, sound or movement

Food service industry

Robots are used to serve people food in some restaurants.

Robot waiters can greet customers, take their order, serve food and clear up dishes.

Robots can also be found preparing food in restaurants or food stalls.

Healthcare

The use of robots in healthcare is growing.

Robots can help surgeons perform operations. In the future, they may perform entire operations themselves.

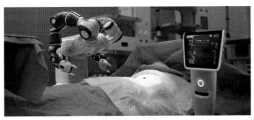

In the healthcare system, robotic limbs can be used to assist people who have been injured or who are disabled.

A robotic arm allows a person to pick up and hold on to objects. Robotic hands can twist to open objects such as jars and doors.

Care robots help to provide care and assistance to patients.

- They may record a patient's temperature, blood pressure and heart rate.
- They may provide the patient with information or even deliver medication to patients.

Care robots may also be created to clean and sanitise hospitals and healthcare facilities.

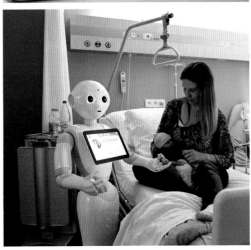

Practise

1 What is each robot doing? Match each letter below to the number of the picture that represents the robot's action.

  A This robot is sorting food.

  B This robot is delivering packages on the ground.

  C This robot is driving a car while the passenger is reading.

  D This robot is preparing a hot drink.

  E This robot is delivering packages by air.

  F This robot is packing boxes that have been sold on a website.

2 State whether the following statements are true or false:

  a A self-driving car is also called an AV.

  b It is too dangerous to use robots for brain surgery.

  c A bus always needs a human driver.

  d Packages can only be delivered using robot drones.

  e Robots preparing food must look like humans.

3 Match each letter below to the number of the picture that represents the robot's action.

A This robot is preparing food.

B This robot is serving food.

C This robotic limb can increase mobility for people with disabilities.

D This robot can care for patients by lifting them.

E This robot can perform surgery.

F This robot can give information to patients.

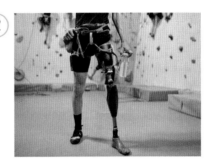

4 State whether the following statements are true or false:

a Robots cannot work in hospitals.

b Robots can make dishes of food.

c There are robots that can perform surgeries on patients.

d Taking a patient's temperature cannot be done by robots.

e Robots cannot serve drinks.

Go further

1 Which statement is **not** true about robots in industry and healthcare?

 a Robots cannot perform surgery.

 b Robots can deliver packages by land or air.

 c Robots are good at giving people information.

 d Robots can serve as waiters in restaurants.

2 Copy the sentences. Fill in the blanks using the words from the word bank below.

 a Robots can function as _____ or _____ in a restaurant.

 b _____ robots can assist nurses and patients by performing certain tasks.

 c E-commerce companies use robot _____ drones to send packages to their customers.

 (delivery)   (chefs)   (healthcare)   (waiters)

3 Work with a partner. Draw a comic strip showing a robot delivering a package to a home. Explain how the package is delivered by the robot.

4 You have learnt what a robot is, as well as what it can and cannot do. Present a short written summary of this topic in 100 words.

Challenge yourself!

1 Pia goes on holiday and stays at a hotel. She is greeted by a robot that gives her information about the activities that she can enjoy at the hotel. The robot was designed by a computer scientist. The hotel is part of the hospitality industry. Can you think of at least two other places or industries where this type of robot might be useful? Discuss with your partner.

2 Using the internet, list two other service industries not covered in this unit.

3 Research one other job from each of the service industries that you listed in question **2** that needs to be done by a computer scientist.

4 What kind of skills do computer scientists need to have?

5 Can you link the topics you have studied in Primary Computing to any of the roles that computer scientists perform?

My project

1 Sanchia says she wants to become a computer scientist.
   - List at least two industries that Sanchia can work in when she becomes a computer scientist.
   - What are some of the tasks that Sanchia might perform in her role as a computer scientist?

   Create a brochure that explains to Sanchia all the things listed above.

2 Maris wants to design robots for the food service industry.
   Research how robots are currently being used in the food service industry.

   Create a table showing the type of robots that work in the food service industry and what each one does. Draw or print out some examples of robots performing these tasks that you find while doing your research.

What can you do?

Read and review what you can do.
- ✔ I know about some of the roles of a computer scientist.
- ✔ I know about some of the roles of robots in service industries.

Great work! You now understand some of the roles of computer scientists and robots!

Unit 6 Be a musician

Making music

Get started!

In groups of three, discuss how repetition is used in the song 'Head, Shoulders, Knees and Toes'.

1 Take turns singing the song and pointing to the body part.
2 Identify the words that are repeated in the song.
3 How many times are the words repeated?
4 Identify which sentence is repeated.
5 How many times is this sentence repeated?

Lyrics:

Head, shoulders, knees and toes, knees and toes.

Head, shoulders, knees and toes, knees and toes.

And eyes, and ears, and mouth, and nose.

Head, shoulders, knees and toes, knees and toes.

March, march, march, let us all march.

March, march, march, get your body charged.

In this unit, you will create music with repetition using Scratch.

You will learn:

- to predict the outcome of algorithms that contain repetition
- to compare and contrast algorithms designed for the same task
- to develop programs with iteration.

Warm up

Work in pairs. Look at the patterns of the musical notes below. Copy the patterns and fill in the blanks to complete the series. Use the following notes:

Do you remember?

Before starting this unit, check that you:
- can follow, understand and correct an algorithm that uses iteration
- can develop a program with the repeat command
- know how to add comments to blocks of code.

In this unit, you will use Scratch.
There is an online chapter all about Scratch.

From algorithm to code
Predicting outcomes

Learn

Repetition in Scratch uses either the forever loop or the repeat loop.

Algorithm A: Saxophone with forever loop

Step	Instruction
1	Start program when any key is pressed
2	Play sound **C Sax** until done
3	Play sound **D Sax** until done
4	Play sound **F Sax** until done
5	Repeat steps 2 to 4 forever
6	Stop program by clicking **Stop** button

Algorithm B: Keyboard with repeat loop

Step	Instruction
1	Start program when sprite is clicked
2	Set volume to 50 %
3	Play sound **E Elec Piano** until done
4	Play sound **F Elec Piano** until done
5	Change volume by 10
6	Repeat steps 3 to 5 five more times
7	Stop program

Look at the steps for Algorithm A and Algorithm B. We can predict the outcome of each algorithm.

Algorithm A with forever loop

This algorithm uses the **Saxophone** sprite.

1   When any key is pressed, the saxophone plays the C sound followed by the D sound then the F sound.

2   The saxophone will continue to play these sounds forever. The program will only stop when the stop button is clicked.

Algorithm B with repeat loop

This algorithm uses the **Keyboard** sprite.

1   When the **Keyboard** sprite is clicked, it plays the E sound and F sound at a volume of 50 %.

2   The volume is then increased by 10.

3   The piano then plays the same sounds again but louder.

4   This continues until the E and F sounds are played six times.

> Remember, in a forever loop, instructions are repeated over and over without stopping. In a repeat loop, instructions are repeated a set number of times.

Practise

1 In pairs, look at the steps in Algorithm C and D.

   a Which algorithm uses the forever loop?

   b Which algorithm uses the repeat loop?

   c Which musical instrument is used in each algorithm?

   d How many times is the **High Tom** sound played in Algorithm C?

   e What is the lowest volume in Algorithm D?

In Scratch, each sprite can play different sounds. Here is the play sound block for the drum:

Algorithm C

Step	Instruction
1	Start program when the **a** key is pressed
2	Set instrument to drum
3	Play sound **Low Tom** until done
4	Wait for $\frac{1}{4}$ second
5	Play sound **High Tom** until done
6	Wait for $\frac{1}{4}$ second
7	Repeat steps 3 to 6 forever
8	Stop program by clicking **Stop** button

Algorithm D

Step	Instruction
1	Start program when Green Flag is clicked
2	Set instrument to electric guitar
3	Set volume to 100 %
4	Play sound **C Elec Guitar** until done
5	Play sound **E Elec Guitar** until done
6	Play sound **A Elec Guitar** until done
7	Play sound **G Elec Guitar** until done
8	Change volume by −10
9	Repeat steps 4 to 8 seven more times
10	Stop program

The minus sign in front of '10' means the volume **decreases** by 10.

Comparing algorithms

The musical note symbols for the 'Baa Baa Black Sheep' song are:

C	C	G	G	A	A	A	A	G
BAA	BAA	BLACK	SHEEP	HAVE	YOU	AN -	Y	WOOL

We want to repeat the song until the space key is pressed. Look at the two Algorithms E and F.

Algorithm E

Step	Instruction
①	Start program when Green Flag is clicked
②	Play C
③	Play C
④	Play G
⑤	Play G
⑥	Play A
⑦	Play A
⑧	Play A
⑨	Play A
⑩	Play G
⑪	Repeat steps 2 to 10 forever
⑫	Stop program

Algorithm F

Step	Instruction
①	Start program when Green Flag is clicked
②	Play C
③	Repeat step 2 one more time
④	Play G
⑤	Repeat step 4 one more time
⑥	Play A
⑦	Repeat step 6 three more times
⑧	Play G
⑨	Repeat steps 2 to 8 until space key is pressed
⑩	Stop program

Let's compare both algorithms. We can say that Algorithm F is best suited for playing the song. Algorithm F has a total of ten steps and repeats the song until the space key is pressed. Whereas Algorithm E has a total of twelve steps and plays the song forever.

Practise

1 The musical note symbols for 'If You're Happy and You Know It' are:

♪C	♪C	♪F	♪F	♪F	♪F	♪F	♪F	♪E	♪F	♩G
IF	YOU'RE	HAP - PY	AND	YOU	KNOW	IT	CLAP	YOUR	HANDS	

a Copy and complete Algorithms G and H.

Step	Instruction – Algorithm G
1	Start program when Green Flag is clicked
2	Play ♪ ____
3	Play ♪ ____
4	Play ♪ ____
5	Play ♪ ____
6	Play ♪ ____
7	Play ♪ ____
8	Play ♪ ____
9	Play ♪ ____
10	Play ♪ ____
11	Play ♪ ____
12	Play ♩ ____
13	Repeat steps 2 to 12 one more time
14	Stop program

Step	Instruction – Algorithm H
1	Start program when Green Flag is clicked
2	Play ♪ ____
3	Repeat step 2 ____ more time
4	Play ♪ ____
5	Repeat step 4 ____ more times
6	Play ♪ ____
7	Play ♪ ____
8	Play ♩ ____
9	Repeat steps 2 to 8 forever
10	Stop program

Remember: a ♪ plays for half a beat, a ♩ plays for one beat, and ♩ plays for two beats.

2 Work in pairs. Compare Algorithm G and Algorithm H.
  a How many steps are there in each algorithm?
  b Which algorithm is best suited to play the song forever?

Using iteration

Iteration means repeating the same block of code over and over again multiple times. There are two types of iteration:

1 **Count-controlled loop** – you have learnt about this in Unit 4

2 Condition-controlled loop.

> **Keyword**
> **condition-controlled loop:** blocks of code are repeated until a condition is met

In Scratch, the **repeat until** block is used to create programs with iteration. It is found under the **Control** group of blocks. We will use condition-controlled loops to make different sounds.

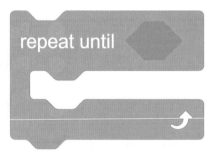

repeat until

Algorithm using iteration

The algorithm below shows the steps to play the snare drum for a quarter of a beat. The snare drum plays repeatedly when the sprite is clicked. The sound stops when the space key is pressed.

Step	Instruction
1	Start program when sprite is clicked
2	Play snare sound **tap snare**
3	Wait 1 second
4	Repeat steps 2 and 3 until the space key is pressed
5	Stop program

Creating a program using iteration

1 Create a new project in Scratch.
2 Add the **Drum-snare** sprite.
3 From the **Events** group, add the **when this sprite clicked** block.
4 From the **Control** group, connect the **repeat until** block to the **when this sprite clicked** block.
5 From the **Sensing** group, insert the **key (space) pressed?** block in the **repeat until** block.

Drum-snare

> The **key (space) pressed?** block lets you choose other keys too.

6 From the **Sound** group, add the **start sound ( )** block inside the **repeat until** block. Click on the dropdown arrow and select **tap snare**.
7 From the **Control** group, add the **wait ( ) seconds** block inside the **repeat until** block. The current value is 1 second.

> The **key (space) pressed?** block is added inside the **repeat until** block.

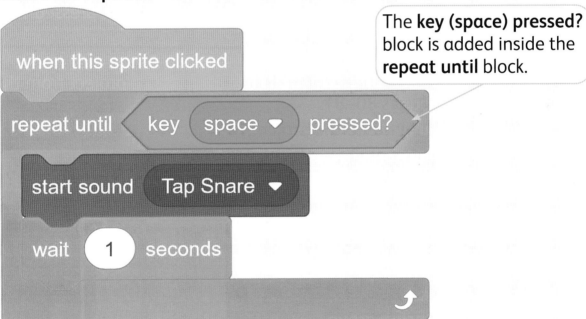

8 Click on the sprite. The snare drum will play the sound **tap snare** and then wait one second. This is repeated.
9 Press the space key to stop the sound. This is a condition-controlled loop.

Practise

1 Take turns to discuss these questions with your partner:

a What does the term 'iteration' mean?

b What is a condition-controlled loop?

c Which blocks in Scratch are used to create programs with iteration?

2 Create a program to play the **sound C2 guitar** on the guitar. The sound should repeat in 2 second intervals when the Green Flag is clicked. The sound should stop when the up-arrow key is pressed.

a Copy and complete the algorithm by filling in the blanks.

Step	Instruction
1	Start program when _____
2	Start sound _____
3	Wait _____ seconds
4	Repeat steps _____ and _____ until the _____ key is pressed
5	Stop program

b Code the algorithm using Scratch as follows. Use the project from the **Learn** panel on pages 80–81.

i Add a **Guitar** sprite to the project.

ii From the **Events** group, add the **when** 🏴 **clicked** block.

iii From the **Control** group, connect the **repeat until** block to the **when** 🏴 **clicked** block.

iv From the **Sensing** group, insert the **key (space) pressed?** block in the **repeat until** block. Click on the drop-down arrow and select **up arrow**.

    v   From the **Sound** group, add the **start sound** block inside the **repeat until** block. Click on the drop-down arrow and select **C2 guitar**.

   vi   From the **Control** group, add the **wait seconds** block to the **start sound** block. Change the number of seconds from **1** to **2**.

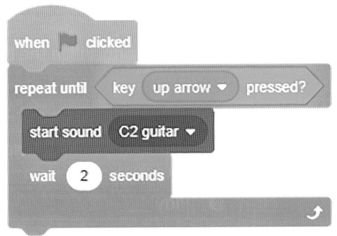

  vii   Click the Green Flag to start the program.

 viii Press the up-arrow key to stop the program.

Go further

The musical note symbols for 'Twinkle Twinkle Little Star' song are:

G	G	D	D	E	E	D
TWIN	- KLE	TWIN	- KLE	LIT	- TLE	STAR

1   Copy and complete Algorithms I and J for the song. Fill in the blanks.

Algorithm I

Step	Instruction
1	Start program when sprite is clicked
2	Play ____
3	Play ____
4	Play ____
5	Play ____
6	Play ____
7	Play ____
8	Play ____
9	Repeat steps 2 to 8 forever
10	Stop program

Algorithm J

Step	Instruction
1	Start program when sprite is clicked
2	Play ____
3	Repeat step 2 ____ more time/s
4	Play ____
5	Repeat step 4 ____ more time/s
6	Play ____
7	Repeat step 6 ____ more time/s
8	Play ____
9	Repeat steps 3 to 8 three more times
10	Stop program

2   Compare and contrast both algorithms.

a   How many steps are there in each algorithm?

b   Which algorithm is best suited to play the song repeatedly four times?

3 Look at the steps for Algorithm K.

  a Which loop does the algorithm use?

  b Predict the outcome of Algorithm K.

  Algorithm K – for **Drums Tabla** sprite

Step	Instruction
1	Start program when **w** key is pressed
2	Set volume to 40 %
3	Play sound **Lo Geh Tabla** until done
4	Play sound **Hi Na Tabla** until done
5	Wait 1 second
6	Play sound **Hi Tun Tabla** until done
7	Change volume by 5
8	Repeat steps 3 to 7 until the down-arrow key is pressed
9	Stop program

4 Create the program for Algorithm K in Scratch.

  a Create a new project.

  b Delete **Sprite1** and add the sprite named **Drums Tabla**.

  c Add the **when (space) key pressed** block to the programming area. Select 'w' from the dropdown menu.

  d Add the **set volume to ()** block. Change the number to 40.

  e Add the **repeat until** block.

  f Press the **down arrow** key to stop the program.

  g Add the **key (space) pressed?** block and select **down arrow**.

  h Add the blocks for steps 3 to 7 inside the **repeat until** block.

  i Add a comment to explain what the code does.

  j Press the 'w' key to run the program.

> You will find the **set volume to ( )** and **change volume by ( )** blocks in the **Sound** group.
>
> set volume to 100 %   change volume by -10

Challenge yourself!

Maggie is singing opera at a concert. Look at Algorithms L and M.

1 Predict the outcome of each algorithm. What is the final volume of Algorithm M?

Algorithm L

Step	Instruction
1	Start program when Green Flag is clicked
2	Set volume to 100 %
3	Play sound **Singer1** until done
4	Wait $\frac{1}{2}$ second – this will be `wait 1 seconds` in Scratch
5	Play sound **Singer2** until done
6	Wait 1 second
7	Change volume by −10
8	Repeat steps 3 to 7 forever
9	Stop program

Algorithm M

Step	Instruction
1	Start program when Green Flag is clicked
2	Set volume to 30 %
3	Play sound **Singer2** until done
4	Wait 1 second
5	Play sound **Singer1** until done
6	Wait 1 second
7	Change volume by 15
8	Repeat steps 3 to 7 two more times
9	Stop program

2 Compare and contrast both algorithms.

   a How many steps are there in each algorithm?

   b Which algorithm is best suited for Maggie repeating the song three times?

3 Rewrite Algorithm M. Name it **Algorithm N** and edit it so that:

   a Maggie will start singing when the sprite is clicked.

   b Maggie continues singing until the key 's' is pressed.

4 Code the program for Algorithm N using Scratch.

   a Create a new project named **Opera**.

   b Delete **Sprite1** and add the sprite **Singer1**.

   c Add the **Theater** Backdrop.

   d Add blocks of code to the programming area.

   e Click on the **Singer1** sprite to start the program.

   f Press the 's' key to stop the program.

> To get the **Singer1** sound, go to the **Sounds** tab and click **Choose A Sound**. Type **Singer1** in the search bar and click to select it. Repeat for the **Singer2** sound.

My project

Let's create a music band with different instruments.

1 Look at the steps in Algorithm P and predict the outcome.

Algorithm P – for **Drum-Highhat** sprite

Step	Instruction
❶	Start program when **up arrow** key is pressed
❷	Set volume to 100 %
❸	Play sound **hihat cymbal** until done
❹	Wait 1 second
❺	Repeat steps 3 and 4 two more times
❻	Stop program

2 We want the backdrop to change brightness repeatedly in 1 second intervals. This should repeat until the 's' key is pressed. Compare Algorithms Q and R. Which algorithm is best suited to this task?

Algorithm Q

Step	Instruction
❶	Start program when Green Flag is clicked
❷	Set brightness to 0
❸	Change brightness by 10
❹	Wait 1 second
❺	Change brightness by –10
❻	Wait 1 second
❼	Repeat steps 3 to 6 until **s** key is pressed
❽	Stop program

Algorithm R

Step	Instruction
❶	Start program when Green Flag is clicked
❷	Set brightness to 0
❸	Change brightness by 5
❹	Wait $\frac{1}{2}$ second
❺	Change brightness by –5
❻	Wait 1 second
❼	Repeat steps 3 to 6 forever
❽	Stop program

3 Write a program using Scratch, as follows:

  a Create a new project and give it a name.

  b Add a backdrop from the music group.

  c Add the sprites: **speaker**, **drum-highhat**, **drum-cymbal**, **guitar-electric**, and **microphone**.

  d When the Green Flag is clicked, program the **speaker** to play the **Drum Jam** sound.

  e Use Algorithm P to program the **drum-highhat** sprite.

  f When the **a** key is pressed, program the **guitar-electric** to start sound **F Elec Guitar**.

  g Add a comment to the code for each sprite explaining what it does.

  h The **microphone** and **drum-cymbal** will remain as static objects.

  i Run your code.

Check that you have completed all tasks. Check what happens when you press:

- the Green Flag

- the up arrow

- the 'a' key.

Did you know?

Iteration means repeating something until the correct result is obtained.
Iteration is used in the real world.

When you eat food you:

- pick up a piece of food
- put it in your mouth
- chew the food
- swallow the food.

If you still feel hungry after
eating a piece of food,
then you repeat these steps.
You keep repeating these steps until you feel full.
Here is another example.

- A chef adds a little salt to cooking and tastes it. He repeats this process
  until the dish tastes just right.

What can you do?

Read and review what you can do.

- ✔ I can predict the outcome of algorithms
  with repetition.
- ✔ I can compare algorithms to see which
  produces the best outcome.
- ✔ I can create programs using iteration.

Well done! Now you can
create music in Scratch!

Database structure

Get started!

This is an example of a completed student record form.

STUDENT RECORD FORM

Student Name	Amir Khan
Date of Birth	January 3, 2011
Age	11 years
Address	Lot 8B New Delhi
Parent's Name 1	Salim Khan
Parent's Name 2	Zara Khan
Contact Number	8476812345
Name of allergies	pollen
Allergies	Yes ❑ No ✔
Transport	Schoolbus ✔ Private car ❑ Other ❑

Discuss with a partner:

1 What is the purpose of the student record form?

2 How many students' information can be collected on one student record form?

  a 1   **b** 2   **c** 15

3 One piece of information that is collected on the form is 'Student Name'. What other information is collected on the form?

> In this unit, you will learn about data tables.

You will learn:

- about the parts of a data table: data, records and fields
- about data types
- how to use a database to answer a question.

Warm up

Work in pairs for this activity. Use the circles to group together the same items.

Draw each circle in your notebook. Write the correct items in each circle.

| chocolate | milk | 2 | $15.00 | Monday, 6 March 2021 | No |

| $0.50 | 62 | 23/06/2021 | 45 | butter | Yes | 8.00 a.m. |

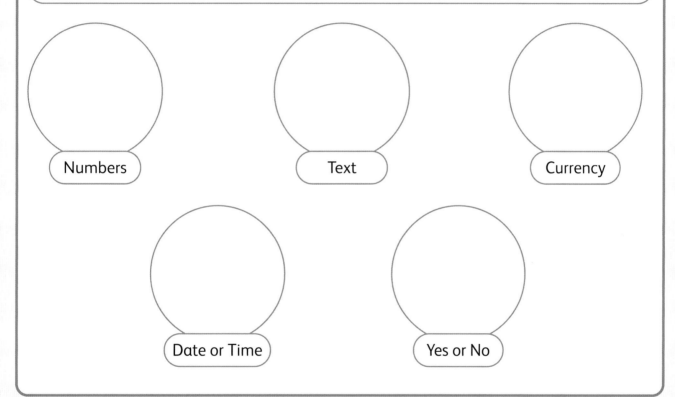

Numbers   Text   Currency

Date or Time   Yes or No

Do you remember?

Before starting this unit, check that you:
- know that questions can be answered using a data table
- can enter data into cells of a spreadsheet
- can format cells
- know the differences between a physical and digital database
- know differences between data and information
- know how to sort data.

Databases
Parts of a data table – data, records, fields

A data table is a collection of data about something. A data table is divided into rows and columns. There can be one data table or several data tables in a database.

Each column represents a **field**. A field holds a single piece of data in a record. There are five fields in this data table. The first field is called 'Patient Name'.

5 fields (columns)

Patient Name	Date of Birth	Age	Allergies	Immunisation
Bill Matthews	03/08/2000	21	No	All
Jessica Layne	15/10/1999	22	No	Some
Simran Khan	04/05/2005	16	Yes	All
Kim Chen	21/11/2010	11	Yes	None

4 records (rows)

data

Each row represents a record.
A **record** is a collection of fields about the same person or object.

Data items is the facts and figures entered in each field for each record.

There are four patients' data in this data table, which means there are four records.

For example, the first record contains all the data for Bill Matthews. The second record contains all the data for Jessica Layne, and so on.

Whose data is stored in the fourth record?

Practise

1 Label the parts of the data table using the words: **data item**, **record**, **field**

A

Item Name	Section	Item Price	Original Quantity	Quantity Sold
Milk	Dairy	$5.00	300	150
Cheese	Dairy	$10.00	100	75
Tomatoes	Produce	$5.50	250	150
Rice	Grain	$12.00	350	200
Red beans	Canned	$4.50	200	100
Soda	Beverage	$2.75	285	125

C

B

2 a How many fields are in the data table?

 b List the names of the fields in the data table.

 c How many records are in the data table?

3 Copy and complete the sentences with the correct words.

(data) (record) (table) (database)

 a A data table is the basic unit of a _____.

 b Data is organised in rows and columns in a data _____.

 c A field holds a single piece of _____ in a record.

 d A _____ is a collection of fields about the same person or object in a database.

Databases
Data types

Each column in a data table represents a unique field. Each field has its own data type. The data type is the kind of data the field can store.

There are four different data types:

- **Text:** Made up of letters or other characters
- **Number:** Can only contain numbers
- **Date/Time:** Contains the date or time
- **Yes/No:** Can only contain one of two values, either 'Yes' or 'No'.

Look at the following table:

Patient information data table

6 fields

Patient Name	Date of Birth	Age	Telephone Number	Allergies	Insurance
Bill Matthews	03/08/2000	21	412-012-4567	No	Yes
Jessica Layne	15/10/1999	22	412-022-1245	No	Yes
Simran Khan	04/05/2005	16	413-256-9988	Yes	No
Kim Chen	21/11/2010	11	413-122-3695	Yes	No

Here are the data types for each field:

- Patient's Name. Data type: **Text**.
- Date of Birth. Data type: **Date/Time**.
- Age. Data Type: **Number**.
- Telephone Number. Data Type: **Text**.
  Note: The data type is not **Number** because this field contains hyphens. The data type **Number** can ONLY store numbers.
- Allergies. Data Type: **Yes/No**.
- Insurance. Data Type: **Yes/No**.

There are rules about what you can do with each data type.

For example, if you want to add two pieces of data, then the data type must be **Number**. Calculations cannot be performed on the data type **Text**.

The table below shows the field name, data type and an example of data from the 'Patient information' data table:

Field name	Data type	Example
Patient name	Text	Simran Khan
Date of birth	Date/Time	04/05/2005
Age	Number	16
Contact number	Text	413-256-9988
Allergies	Yes/No	Yes
Insurance	Yes/No	No

Do you remember why 'Contact number' has a data type of **Text** instead of **Number**?

Think about another field that could be added to the data table. What would be the data type for this field?

Did you know?

When entering data in a field, the data type and format of the data must be the same throughout the data table!

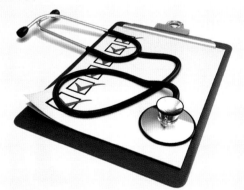

Keywords

data type: the values a field can store

format: the way in which something is arranged

Practise

1 State whether the following statements are true or false:
   a Each column in a data table represents a unique field.
   b Calculations cannot be performed on data that is of type **Text**.
   c Some fields can hold data in different formats.
   d A field with data type **Text** can only store letters.
   e A field with a data type of **Yes/No** can store data with many possible values.

2 Use this data table to answer the questions below.

Student Name	Date of Birth	Contact Number	Outstanding Library Fee	Member of School Clubs	Pick-up Time
Alisha Greene	13/07/2015	222-123-4567	$5.00	No	2:30 p.m.
Mark Simmons	05/09/2014	222-022-1245	$3.00	Yes	3:00 p.m.
Hanna Ali	05/05/2015	222-256-9988	$0.00	No	2:30 p.m.
Zhang Li	20/11/2016	222-122-3695	$0.00	Yes	3:30 p.m.

What is the data type of each field? Choose the correct data type.

(Number) (Text) (Currency) (Date/Time) (Yes/No)

   a Student Name
   b Contact Number
   c Member of School Clubs
   d Date of Birth
   e Pick-up Time

3 Identify another field in the data table above. What is the data type of the field?

Remember the hint given in the **Learn** panel about 'Contact Number'.

Databases
Searching for answers

Information from a database is often used to answer questions.

For example, a shopkeeper may need to know the price of an item. The question she may ask is:

'What is the cost of a tin of red beans?'

To answer this question, a search must be performed in the supermarket's database to find the required data.

One way to find data is to manually search through the database.

Let's look at how we can find the answers to questions using a database.

The database below shows the information for each item sold at a supermarket.

Item Name	Section	Item Price	Original Quantity	Quantity Sold
Milk	Dairy	$5.00	300	150
Cheese	Dairy	$10.00	100	75
Tomatoes	Produce	$5.50	250	150
Rice	Grain	$12.00	350	200
Red Beans	Canned	$4.50	200	100
Soda	Beverage	$2.75	285	125

We will use this database to answer the questions on page 98.

Keyword
search: to look for

Question: How many **Dairy** items are there?

Step 1: Look for the field that has the word 'Dairy'. The field is **Section**.

Step 2: Count the number of times the word 'Dairy' is seen.

Item Name	Section	Item Price	Original Quantity	Quantity Sold
Milk	Dairy	$5.00	300	150
Cheese	Dairy	$10.00	100	75
Tomatoes	Produce	$5.50	250	150
Rice	Grain	$12.00	350	200
Red Beans	Canned	$4.50	200	100
Soda	Beverage	$2.75	285	125

Answer: There are two dairy items.

Question: Which items are in the Dairy section?

Step 1: Look for the field that has the word 'Dairy'. The field is **Section**.

Step 2: Look for the items in the **Item Name** field that matches the word 'Dairy' in the **Section** field.

Item Name	Section	Item Price	Original Quantity	Quantity Sold
Milk	Dairy	$5.00	300	150
Cheese	Dairy	$10.00	100	75
Tomatoes	Produce	$5.50	250	150
Rice	Grain	$12.00	350	200
Red Beans	Canned	$4.50	200	100
Soda	Beverage	$2.75	285	125

Answer: Milk and cheese are the dairy items.

Practise

Use this table to perform searches and answer the questions.

	Student Name	Age	Name of Club	Meeting Time
1	**Student Name**	**Age**	**Name of Club**	**Meeting Time**
2	Alisha Greene	12	Chess	3:00 p.m.
3	Mark Simmons	15	Robotics	3:30 p.m.
4	Hanna Ali	16	Robotics	3:30 p.m.
5	Zhang Li	15	Chess	3:00 p.m.

1 How many students are in the Chess club?

  a One

  b Two

  c Three

2 Which students have a meeting time of 3:30 p.m.?

  a Mark Simmons and Alisha Greene

  b Alisha Greene and Zhang Li

  c Hanna Ali and Mark Simmons

3 Which fields did you look at to answer question **2**?

  a Student Name and Age

  b Age and Meeting Time

  c Name of Club and Meeting Time

  d Meeting Time and Student Name

4 Which club is Hanna Ali in?

  a Robotics

  b Chess

5 Which fields did you look at to answer question **4**?

  a Student Name and Age

  b Student Name and Name of Club

  c Name of Club and Time

  d Meeting Time and Student Name

Go further

Work in pairs. Use the data table below to answer the questions that follow.

	A	B	C	D	E	F
1	Title of Book	Classification	Borrowed By	Date Borrowed	Outstanding	Late Fee
2	Charlotte's Web	Fiction	Sandy Moore	5/10/2021	No	$ -
3	Matilda	Fiction	David Beckles	16/10/2021	Yes	$1.00
4	Harriet The Spy	Mystery	Shria Gomez	14/10/2021	No	$ -
5	One Beam of Light	Science	Judy Chance	10/10/2021	Yes	$2.00

1 a How many records are in the data table?

   b How many fields are in the data table?

2 Match the data types with the fields.

(Number) (Text) (Currency) (Date/Time) (Yes/No)

   a Title of Book

   b Classification

   c Date Borrowed

   d Outstanding

   e Late Fee

3 Perform searches to answer these questions.

   a How many books are classified as 'Science'?

      i   One

      ii Two

      iii Three

   b What are the names of the **Outstanding** books?

      i   'Matilda' and 'Charlotte's Web'

      ii 'Charlotte's Web' and 'Harriet the Spy'

      iii 'Matilda' and 'One Beam of Light'

Challenge yourself!

Use the data table below to answer the questions that follow.

Pizza Order	Size	Cost	Name of Customer	Address	Delivery Time
Cheese	Large	$70.00	Hana Jones	10B Abbey Street	6:00 p.m.
Hawaiian	Medium	$60.00	Sadah Remy	12A Dawson Street	4:00 p.m.
Hawaiian	Large	$90.00	Ken George	101 Park Avenue	4:15 p.m.

1   a   Write the names of the fields in your notebook.

   b   For each field, state the data type.

> Remember, the data types are: numbers, text, currency, date/time, yes/no.

   c   How many records are in the data table?

2   Perform searches to answer these questions:

   a   How many people ordered the Hawaiian pizza?

   b   Who ordered a large pizza?

3   Which fields did you look at to answer question **2b**?

My project

Work in pairs.

There are three paper-based records with travellers' flight details.

1 Draw the data table and use the records below to fill in the table with each traveller's details.

Name	Number of People	Destination	Date of Flight	Cost of Ticket

Travel Details

Name: Sara Lee

Number of People: 1

Destination: Singapore

Date of Flight: 05/06/2021

Cost of Ticket: $950.00

Travel Details

Name: Jane Doe

Number of People: 2

Destination: Miami

Date of Flight: 20/05/2021

Cost of Ticket: $900.00

Travel Details

Name: Damien Charles

Number of People: 2

Destination: Mumbai

Date of Flight: 06/07/2021

Cost of Ticket: $950.00

2 State the data type for each field.

- Name
- Number of People
- Destination
- Date of Flight
- Cost of Ticket

3 a Collect some data about five friends.
Your teacher will give you a spreadsheet file. You can use it to collect the data in a digital format.

b What are the data types for each field?

Name	Age	Month of Birth	Do you like Cats?

4 Copy the data from the table in question **1** to answer these questions:
   a How many people are travelling to Singapore?
   b Which ticket destinations cost $950?
   c Which flight was in May?

What can you do?

Read and review what you can do.
- ✔ I know about data, records and fields.
- ✔ I know about data types for a field.
- ✔ I know how to use a database to answer a question.

Great job! Now you know about data tables, data types and how to use databases to answer questions.

Inventing with code

Get started!

In groups of four, discuss your favourite electronic devices.

1 Talk about the electronic devices you use, for example, mobile phones and tablets.

2 Talk about how data is input into each device, for example, a touchscreen and mouse.

3 Talk about how information is output from each device, for example, screens and speakers.

4 Talk about what you do with each device.

You will learn:

- that decomposition means breaking a task into different parts
- how to identify inputs and outputs
- how to develop a program to produce different outputs from different inputs.

In this unit, you will create programs using the micro:bit.

Warm up

Work in pairs. Look at the patterns below.

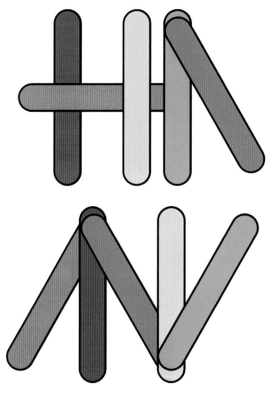
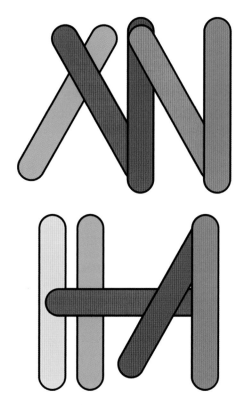

You will need red, orange, yellow, green, blue and purple coloured sticks.

1   Recreate each pattern using the correct coloured sticks.

2   For each pattern, describe the steps you took to create it.

Do you remember?

Before starting this unit, check that you:

- can use logical thinking when creating algorithms
- can follow, understand and correct algorithms with repetition
- can create programs with more than one algorithm
- can create programs to produce an output from an input.

In this unit, you will use MakeCode for micro:bit. There is an online chapter all about MakeCode for micro:bit.

From algorithm to code
Using decomposition

Learn

To solve a problem, you can use decomposition. Decomposition breaks a problem down into smaller parts. We can look at each smaller part to solve the problem.

> **Keyword**
> **decomposition:** a process used to break a task into simpler parts

Creating the algorithms for an emoji badge on micro:bit

We are going to create an emoji badge on the **micro:bit** as follows:

1 Display a happy emoji for 1 second and play the happy sound when **button A** is pressed. This is repeated four times.

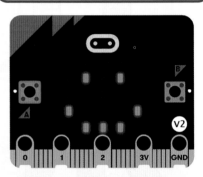

2 Display a sad emoji for 2 seconds and play the sad sound when **button B** is pressed. This is repeated three times.

We can decompose the problem by identifying the components in each algorithm.

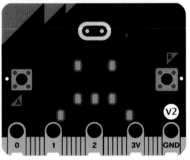

	Component	Algorithm 1	Algorithm 2
①	Which button is used to start the program?	Button A	Button B
②	Which emoji is displayed on the screen?	Happy emoji	Sad emoji
③	How long is the emoji displayed for?	1 second	2 seconds
④	Which sound is played at the same time?	Happy sound	Sad sound
⑤	How many times does the program repeat?	Repeat four times	Repeat three times

Decomposition shows us that we need to write two separate algorithms. We can use the table format to write the algorithms.

The final algorithms are shown below.

Algorithm 1

Step	Instruction
1	Start program when button A is pressed
2	Show happy emoji
3	Play happy sound
4	Wait 1 second
5	Clear screen
6	Wait 1 second
7	Repeat steps 2 to 6 three more times
8	Stop program

Algorithm 2

Step	Instruction
1	Start program when button B is pressed
2	Show sad emoji
3	Play sad sound
4	Wait 2 seconds
5	Clear screen
6	Wait 2 seconds
7	Repeat steps 2 to 6 two more times
8	Stop program

Practise

We want the micro:bit to show multiple emojis as follows:

a Display a surprised emoji for 1 second and play the **spring** sound when **buttons A** and **B** are pressed at the same time. This is repeated two times.

b Display a confused emoji for 5 seconds and play the **twinkle** sound when the **micro:bit** is shaken. This is repeated five times.

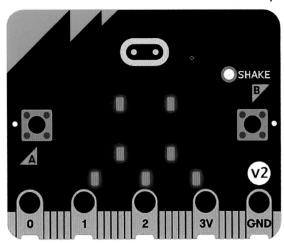
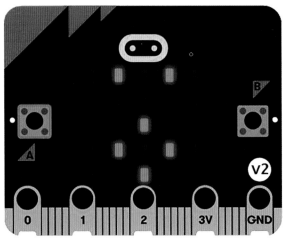

1 Using decomposition, identify the components of each algorithm. Copy and complete the table in your notebook.

Component		Algorithm 1	Algorithm 2
1	What is used to start the program?		
2	Which emoji is displayed on the screen?		
3	How long is the emoji displayed for?		
4	Which sound is played at the same time?		
5	How many times does the program repeat?		

2 Copy the tables below for Algorithms 3 and 4, and fill in the blanks.

Algorithm 3

Step	Instruction
1	Start program when _____ are pressed
2	Show _____ emoji
3	Play _____ sound
4	Wait _____ second
5	Clear screen
6	Wait _____ second
7	Repeat steps 2 to 6 _____ more time/s
8	Stop program

Algorithm 4

Step	Instruction
1	Start program when _____ is shaken
2	Show _____ emoji
3	Play _____ sound
4	Wait _____ seconds
5	Clear screen
6	Wait _____ seconds
7	Repeat steps 2 to 6 _____ more time/s
8	Stop program

3 Can you predict which algorithm in question **2** will take longer to complete when the program is run?

Input and output devices

Just like a computer system, the micro:bit has several built-in input and output devices.

Front of micro:bit	Back of micro:bit
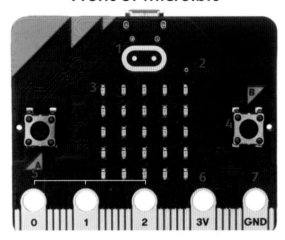	

The input devices include the following:

1 **Touch logo:** The gold micro:bit logo can be programmed to start events when it is touched.

3 **Light sensor:** This measures the level of light. You can program the LEDs to sense, measure and respond to the light level.

4 **Buttons:** There are two buttons, A and B, that you can program.

8 **Radio:** This receives messages sent from another micro:bit.

9 **Temperature sensor:** This measures air temperature.

10 **Accelerometer:** This is a motion sensor. It senses when the micro:bit is tilted forward and backward, left to right, and up and down.

11 **Compass:** This detects magnetic fields. You can program it to show the direction North.

13 **Microphone:** This measures the level of sound.

15 **USB outlet:** This connects to a computer via a USB cable. The computer is used to power the micro:bit and download programs onto it.

17 **Reset/Power button:** This is used to power on the micro:bit or restart your program.

18 **Battery outlet:** This is used to connect a battery pack to power the micro:bit.

The output devices include the following:

2 **Microphone LED:** This turns on when the micro:bit is measuring sound levels.

3 **LED display:** The display has 25 red LEDs. You can program it to display letters, numbers, images or patterns.

6 **3V Pin:** This is used to power external LEDs or devices.

7 **Ground pin:** This is used to complete electrical circuits when headphones or external devices are added to the micro:bit.

8 **Radio:** This sends messages to another micro:bit.

12 **Red power LED:** This turns on when the micro:bit is connected to a power supply (battery pack or computer).

14 **Speaker:** This can program the micro:bit to make different sounds.

16 **Yellow USB LED:** This turns on when the computer is communicating with the micro:bit. For example, the light flashes when a program is downloaded.

> Before coding, it is important that you identify the different input and output devices that you are going to use.

Keywords

input device: a piece of hardware that sends data to the micro:bit

output device: a piece of hardware that allows the micro:bit to send information to us

LED: a small light on the micro:bit

On the micro:bit there are devices that can be programmed to be an input device or an output device. These include the following:

3 **LEDs:** These can be either a light sensor (input device) or an LED display (output device).

8 **Radio:** This can receive (input device) and send messages (output device) wirelessly between micro:bits.

5 **GPIO Pin:** These are used to add input and output devices to the micro:bit. For example, headphones or a buzzer can be added as an output device.

Look at Algorithm 1 for the happy emoji badge on page 106. From the algorithm, we can identify which input and output devices are used.

Input devices:
- Power button
- Button A

Output devices:
- Red power LED
- Speaker
- LED display

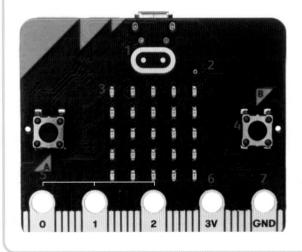

Practise

1 Identify the input/output devices labelled A to M on the micro:bit.

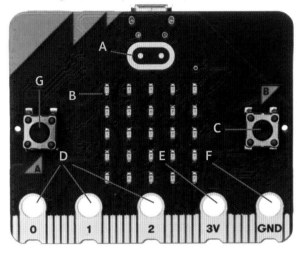 

2 Take it in turns to tell your partner:

   a what each input device does.

   b what each output device does.

3 Look at the algorithm below for making a light turn on and off in time to music played nearby. The louder the sound, the brighter the LEDs.

Step	Instruction
①	Start program when simulator is started
②	Turn on all LEDs on the display
③	Set LED brightness based on sound level
④	Repeat step 3 forever
⑤	Stop program

Identify:

a the input devices.

b the output devices.

Coding on micro:bit

Creating the program for the emoji badge

We will use **Microsoft MakeCode** for **micro:bit** to create programs. Look at the steps below for the happy emoji. It uses two input devices and three output devices.

1 Create a new project named **Emoji Badge**.

2 Delete the **on start** and **forever** blocks from the programming area.

3 Go to the **Input** group. Add the **on button pressed** block to the programming area. Select 'A' from the dropdown menu.

4 Go to the **Loops** group. Add the **repeat** block to the **on button pressed** block. The default number of times to repeat is '4'.

5 Go to the **Basic** group. Add the **show icon** block to the **repeat** block. Click on the dropdown arrow and select 'the happy face'.

6 Go to the **Music** group. Add the **play sound** block to the **show icon** block. Click on the dropdown arrow and select 'happy'.

7 Go to the **Basic** group. Add the **pause (ms)** block. Click on the dropdown arrow and select '1 second'.

8 Go to the **Basic** group. Add the **clear screen** block.

9 Add a second **pause (ms)** block. Click on the dropdown arrow and select '1 second'.

10 Click play to start the simulator.

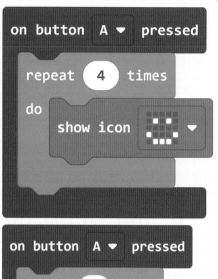

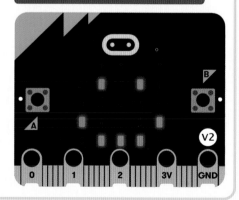

11 Click on button A to run the program.
Save your project.

When button A is pressed, you will hear the happy sound every time the happy emoji is displayed on the LED screen. This is repeated four times in total.

The steps below show how to edit the program to include the sad emoji. The edited program uses three input devices and three output devices.

1   Open your project. Keep the existing code. You will create a second block of code.

2   Go to the **Input** group. Add the **on button pressed** block to the programming area. Select 'B' from the dropdown menu.

3   Go to the **Loops** group. Add the **repeat** block to the **on button pressed** block. Change the number from **4** to **3**.

4   Go to the **Basic** group. Add the **show icon** block to the **repeat** block. Click on the dropdown arrow and select 'the sad face'.

5   Go to the **Music** group. Add the **play sound** block to the **show icon** block. Click on the dropdown arrow and select 'sad'.

6   Go to the **Basic** group. Add the **pause (ms)** block. Click on the dropdown arrow and select '2 seconds'.

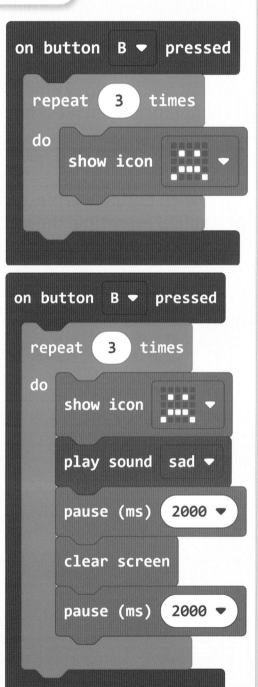

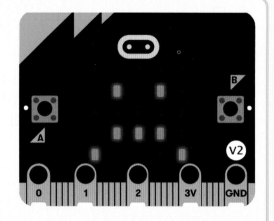

7   Go to the **Basic** group. Add the **clear screen** block.

8   Add a second **pause (ms)** block. Click on the dropdown arrow and select '2 seconds'.

9   Click play to start the simulator.

10 Press button A.

11 Wait for the happy emoji to be displayed four times. Then press button B.

12 Save your project.

When button B is pressed, you will hear the sad sound every time the sad emoji is displayed on the LED screen. This is repeated three times in total.

Practise

1 Identify which group each of the following blocks belong to in **MakeCode**:
   a Play sound
   b Clear screen
   c Repeat
   d On button pressed
   e Show icon
   f Pause (ms)

2 Work in pairs. Use **MakeCode** to create the program for a disco light.
   a Create a new project named **Disco Light**.
   b Go to the **Basic** group. Add the **show leds** block to the **on start** block in the programming area. Turn on all 25 LEDs on the display by clicking on each one.
   c Go to the **LED** group and select **more**. Add the **set brightness** block to the **forever** block in the programming area.
   d Go to the **Input** group. Add the **sound level** block inside of the **set brightness** block.

   e On the simulator, move the sound level slider up and down. You will notice the LEDs get brighter for louder sounds and the LEDs get dimmer for quieter sounds.
   f If you have a **micro:bit** device, download the program onto it. Dim the lights and play some music.

> When a new project is created, the **on start** block and the **forever** block are in the programming area by default.

Go further

Work in pairs to create a name badge using the micro:bit.

a   When button A is pressed, a name scrolls across the display followed by a pitchfork icon. After 500 ms, the screen clears.

b   When button B is pressed, another name scrolls across the display followed by a heart icon. After 500 ms, the screen clears.

Computational thinking

1   Copy these algorithm tables into your notebook. Using decomposition, fill in the blanks for each algorithm. For algorithms a and b, choose two different names of your choice.

a

Step	Instruction
❶	Start program when button ___ is pressed
❷	Show string ___
❸	Show icon ___
❹	Wait ___ ms
❺	Clear ___
❻	Stop program

b

Step	Instruction
❶	Start program when button ___ is pressed
❷	Show string ___
❸	Show icon ___
❹	Wait ___ ms
❺	Clear ___
❻	Stop program

2 From the algorithms identify:

   a the input devices.

   b the output devices.

3 Use **MakeCode** to create the program for a name badge.

   a Create a new project named **Name badge**.

   b Delete the **on start** and **forever** blocks from the programming area.

   c Add the **on button pressed** block to the programming area. Select 'A'.

   d Add the **show string** block from the **Basic** group to the **on button pressed** block. Click on this block and type a name.

   e Add the **show icon** block to the **show string** block. Select the icon of your choice.

   f Add the **pause (ms)** block to the **show icon** block. Select 500 ms.

   g Add the **clear screen** block to the **pause (ms)** block.

   h Add another **on button pressed** block to the programming area. Select 'B'.

   i Repeat steps d to g.

   j Click play to start the simulator.

   k Click on button A. You will see the first name scroll across the screen followed by the icon.

   l When the screen clears, click on button B. You will see the second name scroll across the screen followed by the icon. Save your project.

Challenge yourself!

In this challenge, you will create a program for the micro:bit to be used as a random number selector.

When the micro:bit is shaken, it displays a random number between 1 to 6 on the LED display. This number is shown for 5 seconds and the screen clears.

When the micro:bit logo is touched, it displays a random number between 2 to 12 on the LED display. This number is shown for 2 seconds and the screen clears.

1 Use decomposition to complete the algorithms by filling in the blanks.

a

Step	Instruction
1	Start program when micro:bit is ___
2	Show random ___ between ___ to ___
3	Wait ___ seconds
4	Clear _____
5	Stop program

b

Step	Instruction
1	Start program when logo is ___
2	Show random ___ between ___ to ___
3	Wait ___ seconds
4	Clear _____
5	Stop program

2 Create the program for the random number selector.
   a Create a new project and name it **NumberSelector**.
   b Add the code for the first algorithm to the programming area.
   c Add the code for the second algorithm to the programming area.
   d Click play to start the simulator.
   e Click the shake button on the simulator. A random number between 1 to 6 will appear on the display for 5 seconds.
   f Press the logo. A random number between 2 to 12 will appear on the display for 2 seconds.
   g If you have a physical micro:bit, download the program to it and have fun playing games. If the game requires a number between 1 and 6, shake the micro:bit. If the game requires a number between 2 and 12, press the logo.

> Hint: You will find the **pick random** block in the **Math** group. Insert the **pick random** block in the **show number** block for step 2 of the algorithm.

My project

Turn the **micro:bit** into a pet that makes sounds and shows emotions when it is touched and shaken.

a When the program starts, the pet is asleep (so the **micro:bit** shows a sleep icon).

b When the **micro:bit** is shaken, the pet shows an angry face (displays an angry icon) and makes a soaring sound. The pet then goes back to sleep.

c When the logo is touched, the pet shows a happy face and makes a giggle sound. The pet then goes back to sleep.

Computational thinking

1 Using decomposition, complete the algorithms by filling in the blanks for each part.

a

Step	Instruction
❶	Start program on ___
❷	Show ___ icon
❸	Stop program

b

Step	Instruction
❶	Start program when micro:bit is ___
❷	Show ___ icon
❸	Play ___ sound until done
❹	Show ___ icon
❺	Stop program

This project has three algorithms that are represented as three sections of code on **MakeCode**.

c

Step	Instruction
❶	Start program when logo is ___
❷	Show ___ icon
❸	Play ___ sound until done
❹	Show ___ icon
❺	Stop program

2 From the algorithms, identify which input and output devices are used.

3 Use **MakeCode** to create the program for the pet.
   a Create a new project and give it a name.
   b Add the code for the first algorithm to the programming area.
   c Add the code for the second algorithm to the programming area.
   d Add the code for the third algorithm to the programming area.

You will need this block for the third algorithm.

   e Click play to start the simulator. What do you see on the display?
   f Click the shake button on the simulator. Explain what happens.
   g Click the logo on the simulator. Explain what happens.
4 Edit the code for the second algorithm as follows:
   a When the micro:bit is shaken, the pet shows an angry face and makes a soaring sound twice. The pet then goes back to sleep.
   b Click the shake button on the simulator to see if the edited code works.

Did you know?

The human body has input devices that are the five sense organs:
1 Tongue for taste
2 Skin for touch
3 Eyes for sight
4 Nose for smell
5 Ears for hearing

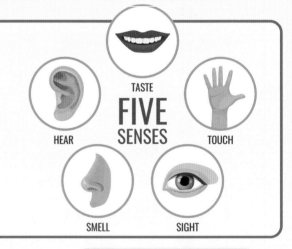

What can you do?

Well done! Now you can create programs on **micro:bit**!

Read and review what you can do.
   ✔ I can create algorithms by using decomposition.
   ✔ I can identify inputs and outputs.
   ✔ I can create programs to produce different outputs from different inputs.

Network failure and encryption

Get started!

Work with a partner to create a secret message to send to a friend in the class.

For example, you could write the words 'TOP SECRET' backwards on a sheet of paper. This will spell 'POT TERCES'.

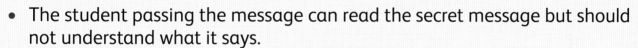

- On a separate sheet of paper, explain how to read the message – for example: 'We must always read in reverse.'

- Pass the explanation to a friend in your class.

- Pass the secret message to another student in your class, to pass on to your friend.

- The student passing the message can read the secret message but should not understand what it says.

Do you think your friend will be able to understand the message without the explanation?

Would the explanation make it easier for your friend to read the message?

Should everyone be able to understand the explanation?

You will learn:
- what happens if a network fails
- about encryption
- about the Caesar and Pigpen ciphers.

In this unit, you will learn about network failure and encryption.

Warm up

Each number in the diagram below represents a letter.

a	b	c	d	e	f	g	h	i	j	k	l	m	n	o	p	q	r	s	t	u	v	w	x	y	z
1	2	3	4	5	6	7	8	9	10	11	12	13	14	15	16	17	18	19	20	21	22	23	24	25	26

1 Work with a partner to complete the word in the table below.

5	14	3	18	25	16	20	9	15	14

   a Do you think this is a good way to create a secret message?

   b Can you suggest ways to improve this method?

2 You can match different numbers with different letters to create a new code. Create another code of your own.

3 Discuss with your partner a method that you could use to send your own secret messages.

Do you remember?

Before starting this unit, check that you:
- know about some things you can do on a network
- know about some advantages and disadvantages of a network
- know what a cipher is
- can use a simple code to write and decode messages.

Networks
Network failure issues

Learn

Network failure is when a fault with hardware or software stops a network working properly.

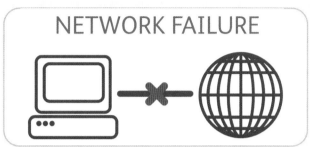

Network failure may affect the whole network. Or it may only affect some services on the network.

Network failure means computers cannot:

- share files
- send emails
- communicate with other users on the network
- access information on the network
- access the internet.

Network failure can have serious effects on organisations that depend on networks.

In schools, teachers would not be able to use online resources to teach lessons.

Students may not be able to access their classes and do online quizzes.

Office staff would not be able to access student information stored on the network.

A network failure in a hospital could lead to patient illness or even death.

Doctors would not be able to access patient files.

It might affect the software they use to care for patients.

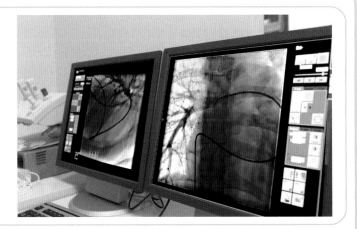

Network failure can prevent police officers from sharing information with colleagues. This can stop them from fighting crime.

In shops, the failure of the network could mean fewer sales and stress for customers and owners.

Can you think of other places where network failure may cause difficulties for the users of the network?

Did you know?

Human error is a leading cause of network failure.

Keyword

network failure: when a network stops working properly due to hardware or software faults

Practise

1 State which of these statements are true or false:
   a Network failure does not disrupt services on a network.
   b Network failure does not affect the earnings of retail businesses.
   c The jobs of police officers can be affected if there is a network failure.

2 Choose the most appropriate answer for each of the following:
   a Network failure can prevent the sharing of _____.
      (emails, electricity, water)
   b Network failure may prevent students from _____.
      (doing homework exercises in their textbooks, viewing videos stored on their computer, doing online quizzes)

3 Give an example of how a network failure may affect a retail business like a supermarket.

4 Give two examples of how network failure can affect hospitals.

5 List two problems a teacher may encounter if the school's network is down.

Encryption

Learn

Encryption means disguising a message so that it can only be understood by certain people.

Encryption uses a key. The key explains how the message has been disguised.

Encrypted data is known as **ciphertext**. Unencrypted data is called **plain text**.

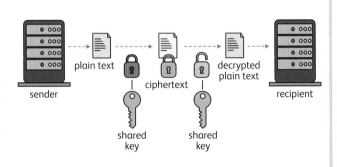

Today, most communication and business takes place over networks and the internet.

Encryption is used in these applications to:

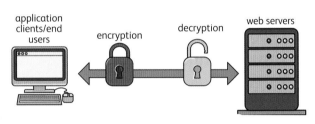

- safely exchange data between web servers and browsers

- withdraw cash from ATMs

- send secure emails

- send online data files, photos, videos, and so on.

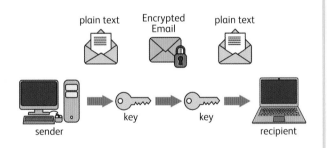

- send messages to friends and family through messenger applications.

Encryption keeps digital data secret while being stored or sent.

Encryption does not stop someone from reading a message – instead it stops them being able to understand it.

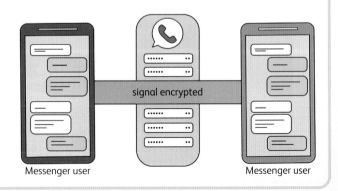

Encryption helps protect data you send, receive and store.

Internet privacy

Encryption is essential to help protect sensitive personal information. To ensure privacy, documents such as spreadsheets, databases and word documents should be encrypted before being sent over the internet.

Protection against hacking

Cybercrime is a global problem. Criminals often try to steal personal information for financial gain.

Purchases made online are encrypted to try to prevent theft of credit card details.

Government Regulations

Many governments have passed laws requiring businesses and other organisations to protect personal information.

For example, schools must protect student records, hospitals must protect patient records and businesses must protect customer information.

Keywords

encryption: disguises data so that only people with access to a secret key can understand it

ciphertext: encrypted data

plain text: refers to data before it is encrypted

cybercrime: criminal activities carried out by means of computers or the internet

Practise

1 State which of the following statements are true or false:

a Encrypted data is commonly referred to as plain text.

b Unencrypted data is called ciphertext.

c Encryption is the process of converting information or data into a code.

d Encryption requires the use of a key for the intended user to understand the message sent.

e Encryption is used to ensure that emails sent over a network are protected from unauthorised persons.

f Messenger messages are not encrypted.

g Encryption can prevent someone from intercepting a message.

h Encryption stops the wrong people from understanding a message they have accessed without permission.

2 Copy the sentences. Choose the correct word to complete the sentences.

(intercepting)　(confidentiality)　(personal)　(hackers)

(key)　(servers)

a An encryption _____ is the secret that explains how a message is coded.

b Encryption is used to protect the _____ of data transmitted over a network or the internet.

c _____ often steal personal information for financial gain.

d Encryption does not prevent someone from _____ a message.

e Encryption helps to safely exchange data between web _____ and browsers.

Write and decode messages
Caesar cipher and Pigpen cipher

Learn

Caesar cipher

One of the oldest methods of encryption is the Caesar cipher.

It works by replacing each plain text letter with a new letter. The new letter is found at the original letter's position in the alphabet plus the value of the key. The key is the number of places each letter was moved. Historically this was usually three.

For example, a key value of three would change the plain text message 'good job' to the ciphertext message 'jrrg mre'.

The ciphertext can be decrypted by applying the same number of shifts in the opposite direction.

This type of encryption is known as a substitution cipher. This is because you substitute one letter for another.

Keyword

decrypt: to convert a code into a form that can be read

131

Did you know?

The Caesar cipher is an example of ancient cryptography and was said to be used by the Roman Emperor Julius Caesar to send private messages.

Practise

1   State whether the following statements are true or false:
    a   The Caesar cipher can be used to encrypt messages.
    b   The Caesar cipher is also known as a substitution cipher.
    c   To encrypt a message using the Caesar cipher, each letter is replaced by another letter a number of places before the letter.

2   Complete the encryption for the following message using the Caesar cipher and a key of 3:

    'I got a new pet'

    A B C D E F G H I J K L M N O P Q R S T U V W X Y Z

Plain text	I		g	o	t		a		n	e	w		p	e	t
Ciphertext	L		J	R	W										

3   Encrypt the same message above, 'I got a new pet', using the Caesar cipher and a key of 5. Compare the answer with the one in question **2** above.

4   Decrypt the following message using the Caesar cipher and a key of 3:

    Vhh brx wrqljkw

5   a   Encrypt the word '**play**' using the Caesar cipher with a key of 4.

    b   What would you do when you reach the last letter of the alphabet? Discuss with your partner.

Learn

Pigpen cipher

The pigpen is a simple substitution cipher that exchanges letters for symbols. The alphabet is written in grids, as shown below.

Encryption involves replacing each letter with a symbol. The symbol is the part of the pigpen grid that contains the letter.

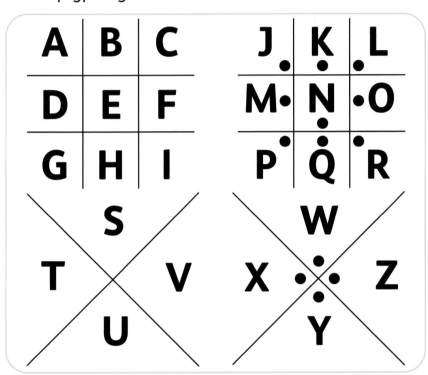

For example, the word 'box' is encrypted as:

Did you know?

The pigpen cipher has been in use since the 1500s.

The decryption process is just the reverse of the encryption process. Using the same key (the grid above), find the image in the ciphertext, and replace it with the letter given by that part of the grid.

What do you think the following code means?

Hint: The first letter is T.

1 Which pigpen symbols would be used to represent the following letters of the alphabet?

A	D	H	K	N	P	T	U	W	Z

2 Encrypt the following statements using the Pigpen cipher:
   a It is sunny
   b I am a hero
   c Here comes the rain
   d The treasure is in the buried chest

3 Decrypt the following:

   a ⌐ ⌊·⌈⊔☐ >⊓☐

   b ⌐ ⌊·⊏∧☐ >⊓☐ ⌐⌋⌈⊡

   c > ⊐⌋⌈⌈·∨ >⊓☐ ∨⌐⌈⊏>

Go further

1 State three issues that may result from network failure.

2 Explain how network failure may affect the police.

3 Explain two problems students may encounter if the school's network is disrupted.

4 Describe how encryption can protect personal information.

5 Work with a partner. Write a secret message in plain text. Convert the message using the Caesar cipher. Use a key of your choice.

6 Decode the following Pigpen cipher:

Challenge yourself!

1 Explain how a network failure may affect a bank.

2 Give three reasons why encryption of data is important.

3 Explain the difference between encryption and decryption.

4 a State three applications where encryption is important.

  b Explain the importance of using encryption in those applications.

5 Explain to your partner how the Caesar cipher method works.

6 a Explain the difference between the Caesar cipher and the Pigpen cipher.

  b Which method do you believe is more secure?

7 A cipher wheel can be used to decrypt messages a lot faster than doing it on paper. Work with a partner to create a Caesar cipher wheel. The list of items that you will need is shown on the next page.

Cardboard: A base on which to attach the two spinning circles for the cipher

Card: To create two spinning circles and attach to the cardboard. One smaller and one larger

Scissors: To cut out the two circles from the card

Ruler: To draw straight lines

Pin: To connect the smaller and bigger cardboard circles so you get the spinning wheel

Pencil: To draw lines and write letters on the cipher wheel

Coloured pencils or pens: You can use different coloured pencils or pens to decorate the cipher wheel.

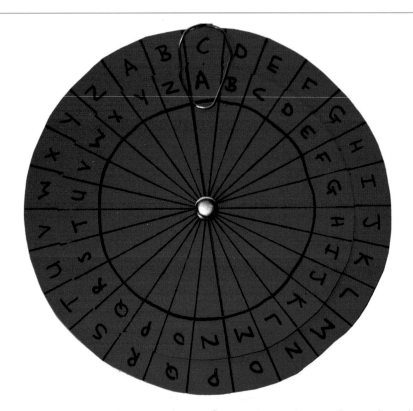

8   Suggest a way to include numbers from 0 to 9 on the wheel.

9   Explain to your partner how it would work.

10 Draw a sketch of a Pigpen cipher wheel on a piece of paper.

11 Explain to your partner how the Pigpen cipher wheel will work.

My project

1 Your school's network is down because of some type of error. Your computer science teacher has asked the class to investigate and write a report about the difficulties the school could face due to network failure.

2 You find out later that the network failed because it had been hacked. However, the data on the network was encrypted. Add a section to your report explaining how encryption works and why it is important.

3 Your teacher would also like students to work with a partner to create a new cipher, using letters, shapes, colours or any other method to send encrypted messages. To test the new cipher, you must do the following:

   a Send a message to a friend in the class using the new cipher. Do not send them the secret key.

   b Check to see if the person receiving the message understands it.

   c Send the message to another friend, but this time also send the secret key. Check to see if this friend understands the message.

What can you do?

Read and review what you can do.

✔ I know about problems that are caused by a network failure.

✔ I know what encryption is.

✔ I know where and why encryption is used.

✔ I can write and decode messages using the Caesar cipher.

✔ I can write and decode messages using the Pigpen cipher.

Well done! You now know about encryption, ciphers and the impact of network failures.

Creating computer games

Get started!

Have you ever played a computer game that seemed to repeat the same thing over and over again?

In small groups, discuss how repetition can be used in the following two types of games:

Sports games

Puzzle games

1 Which parts of these games are repeated?
2 Do the repeated actions make the games fun?
3 How do these games keep you interested in playing?

You will learn:

- about algorithms
- to develop algorithms with repetition
- to test different parts of a program.

In this unit, you will use sub-routines and repetition to create algorithms and computer games in Scratch.

Warm up

Work in pairs. The rat below must take a certain path to get to the cheese. There is a pattern to the path. What is the pattern?

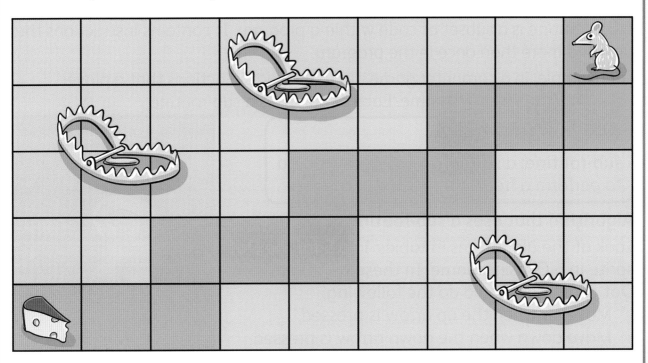

Complete the first two steps that the rat should take to get to the cheese.

> STEP 1: Move _____
> STEP 2: Move _____

How many times must these steps be repeated so the rat gets to the cheese? Discuss with your partner.

Do you remember?

Before starting this unit, check that you:
- can break a task into smaller parts
- can plan a program
- know about loops.

In this unit, you will use Scratch. There is an online chapter all about Scratch.

Understanding sub-routines

Computer programs can contain sub-routines.

A sub-routine is a subset of code within a program. It contains instructions that are used more than once in the program.

For example, in a computer game, there are certain actions that a player repeats throughout the game. Each action uses a sub-routine.

Keyword

sub-routine: a set of instructions designed to perform a frequently-used operation

Algorithm that uses a sub-routine

Look at the algorithms in tables 1 to 5 for the **Dot** sprite in a Chasing Game. In these algorithms, the **Dot** character should do the following:

- Move up when the up arrow is pressed.
- Move down when the down arrow is pressed.
- Move to the left when the left arrow is pressed.
- Move to the right when the right arrow is pressed.

When any of the four arrow keys are pressed, **Dot** should also turn 30 degrees to the right, change costume and bark.

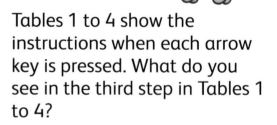

Table 1

Step	Instruction
1	Start program when up arrow key is pressed
2	Change y position by 10
3	Run "Move Around" sub-routine

Tables 1 to 4 show the instructions when each arrow key is pressed. What do you see in the third step in Tables 1 to 4?

Table 2

Step	Instruction
1	Start program when down arrow key is pressed
2	Change y position by −10
3	Run "Move Around" sub-routine

Before creating a computer program with a sub-routine, we can write the algorithm that uses this sub-routine.

Table 3

Step	Instruction
①	Start program when left arrow key is pressed
②	Change x position by –10
③	Run "Move Around" sub-routine

Table 4

Step	Instruction
①	Start program when right arrow key is pressed
②	Change x position by 10
③	Run "Move Around" sub-routine

Table 5

Step	Instruction
①	Start "Move Around" sub-routine
②	Turn 30 degrees to the right
③	Switch to the next costume
④	Play bark sound

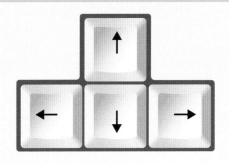

Table 5 shows the steps of the **Move Around** sub-routine. The first step in Table 5 is to define that this is a sub-routine.

Each of the Tables 1 to 4 uses the **Move Around** sub-routine in step 3. Writing this sub-routine means we do not have to add separate instructions to Tables 1 to 4.

Practise

Explain to your partner what the algorithms below do.

Step	Instruction
①	Start program when space key is pressed
②	Say "Oh yeah!"
③	Run "Jump" sub-routine
④	Play pop sound

Step	Instruction
①	Start "Jump" sub-routine
②	Change y position by 50
③	Wait for 0.2 seconds
④	Change y position by –50

Using repetition

Let's summarise what we now know about loops. There are two types of loops:

Loops

- **Indefinite (forever) loops** where instructions repeat without stopping. This is called repetition.

| Definite (repeat) loops – iteration | Indefinite (forever) loops – repetition |

- **Definite (repeat) loops** where instructions repeat a number of times before stopping. This is called iteration.

There are two types of definite (repeat) loops: condition-controlled loops and count-controlled loops.

We looked at algorithms containing count-controlled loops in Unit 4.

In this section, we will develop an algorithm that uses a **Repeat** loop to have characters repeat actions for a known number of times.

Change an algorithm to perform actions using Repeat

Look at the algorithm in the table below for the second character, **Robot**, in the Chasing Game. In this algorithm, the **Robot** character should perform the following actions once:

- Play a sound called **Computer Beep**.
- Say **'You can't catch me!'** for 1 second.
- Glide $\frac{1}{2}$ second to a random position.

Step	Instruction
1	Start program when Green Flag is clicked
2	Set position to: x = 125 y =70
3	Play computer beep sound
4	Say "You can't catch me!" for 1 second
5	Glide $\frac{1}{2}$ second to random position

This algorithm can be changed so the **Robot's** actions are repeated a specific number of times. We can do this by using a **Repeat** loop. In step 6, we use a **Repeat** loop to repeat these instructions a total of eight times.

Step	Instruction
1	Start program when Green Flag is clicked
2	Set position to: x = 125 y = 70
3	Play computer beep sound
4	Say "You can't catch me!" for 1 second
5	Glide $\frac{1}{2}$ second to random position
6	Repeat steps 3 to 5 seven more times

Steps 3, 4 and 5 occur 8 times in total.

Practise

Develop an algorithm that includes repetition for a third character in the Chasing Game. In this algorithm, your character should do the following:

- Start when the **Green Flag** is clicked.
- Play a sound called **Pop** five times at the start.
- Switch to the next costume five times at the start.
- Move 10 steps after the last costume switch.
- Say '**Ha-ha**' three times after moving 10 steps.
- Turn 90 degrees to the left three times after moving 10 steps.

Step	Instruction
1	
2	
3	
4	
5	
6	
7	
8	

Testing programs

Scratch code for the **Dot** character in the Chasing Game is shown below.
We can run this program to check if it matches the algorithm on pages 140–141.

Code for Dot Sprite

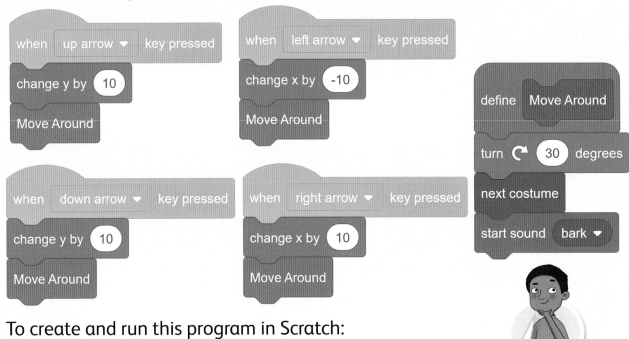

To create and run this program in Scratch:

1 Open a new project.
2 Choose the **Galaxy** Backdrop and the **Dot** sprite.
3 Add the code above to **Dot**.
4 Click the **Green Flag** to start the program.
5 Press the **Up**, **Down**, **Left** and **Right** arrow keys repeatedly to see if you get the desired results.

The **Move Around** block can be created from **My Blocks** in the palette, changing the block name to **Move Around**.

When you run the program, you should notice that it does not do exactly what we want.

This program has an error. **Dot** does not move correctly.

We can test different parts of the program systematically to identify and debug (fix) errors.

This program has five different groups of code. We can click on any block in each group to test that part of the program.

- When we click on the **define Move Around** block, we can check that **Dot** turns 30 degrees to the right, changes costume and plays a bark sound.

- When we click on the **When up arrow key pressed** block, we can check that **Dot** moves up and then runs the **Move Around** sub-routine.

When you test all five parts, you should see that the error is in the **When down arrow key pressed** block of code.

We can fix the error by changing 10 to −10 as shown:

Keyword

systematically: testing in turn until we find the error

Practise

Create the Chasing Game in Scratch.

1 Create the program with the corrected code for the **Dot** sprite.

2 Add the second sprite, **Robot**, to your project.

3 Change the size of both sprites from **100** to **75** on the Stage.

Step	Instruction
1	Start program when Green Flag is clicked
2	Set position to: x = 125 y = 70
3	Play computer beep sound
4	Say "Catch me!" for 2 seconds
5	Go to random position
6	Repeat steps 3 to 5 six more times

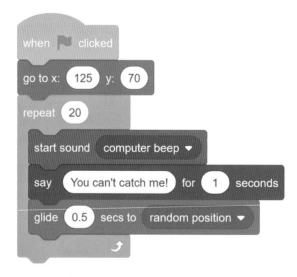

4 Add the code above to the **Robot** sprite.

5 Click the **Green Flag** to run your program.

6 Check if you get the desired results for the **Robot** character. Does the program match the algorithm above?

7 Test the program to identify and debug any errors.

Go further

1 Look at the algorithm below for a character in a computer game.

Monkey: Part 1

Step	Instruction
1	Start program when space key is pressed
2	Switch to the next costume
3	Run "Jump" sub-routine
4	Say "He-he-he" for 1 second

Monkey: Part 2

Step	Instruction
1	Start "Jump" sub-routine
2	Change y position by **40**
3	Wait for 0.2 seconds
4	Change y position by **–40**

Write, in your own words, what the algorithm does.

Computational thinking

Change the algorithm above to repeat the sub-routine action five times.

Look at the code below created for this game.

2 Create this program in Scratch using the **Monkey** sprite and the **Jungle** Backdrop.

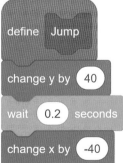
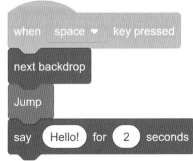

```
define  Jump

change y by  40

wait  0.2  seconds

change x by  -40
```

```
when  space ▼  key pressed

next backdrop

Jump

say  Hello!  for  2  seconds
```

3 Run your program. Does the program match the algorithm above?

4 Test different parts of the program to identify and debug any errors.

Challenge yourself!

Continue creating the computer game from the **Go further** activity.

We want a **Bananas** sprite to turn, glide, play a sound and decrease its size when the sprite is clicked. We also want an **Apple** sprite to go to a random position, play a sound and change its colour six times.

1   Look at the algorithm for the second character **Bananas** in your program.

Bananas: Part 1

Step	Instruction
1	Start program when this sprite is clicked
2	Run "Move Banana" sub-routine
3	Play Bite sound
4	Change size by –10

Bananas: Part 2

Step	Instruction
1	Start "Move Banana" sub-routine
2	Turn 30 degrees to the right
3	Glide 1 second to random position

2   Add the **Bananas** sprite to your project.

3   Add code to the **Bananas** sprite that matches its algorithm.

4   Add the **Apple** sprite.

5   Look at the algorithm below for the third character **Apple** in your game.

Apple: Part 1

Step	Instruction
1	Start program when Green Flag is clicked
2	Run "Move Apple" block
3	Wait for $\frac{1}{2}$ second
4	Repeat steps 2 and 3 six times

Apple: Part 2

Step	Instruction
1	Start "Move Apple" block
2	Go to random position
3	Play Chomp sound
4	Change colour effect by 25

6   Add code to the **Apple** sprite that matches its algorithm.

7   Run your program and check if you get the desired results.

Find and fix any errors by testing different parts of the program.

My project

Create a computer drawing game. When you press the space key, one sprite should draw circles in different colours. When you click on another sprite, it should make five stamps of itself.

1 Create a new project and add the **Pen** extension blocks to the palette.
2 Add the **Beetle** sprite and the code below.
3 Run and test your program.
4 Write the algorithm for this character that matches the code.

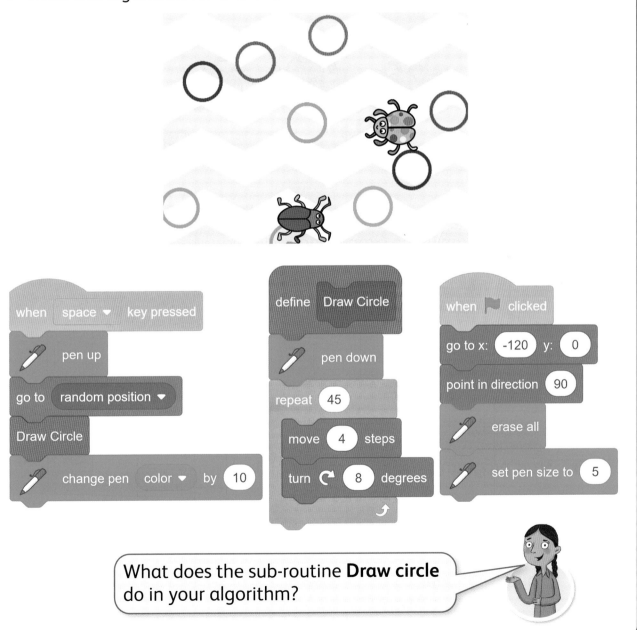

What does the sub-routine **Draw circle** do in your algorithm?

5 Add the **Ladybug1** sprite and the code that will match the algorithm below.

6 Change the algorithm and then the code to have the sprite make a stamp of itself five times.

7 Test and debug your program.

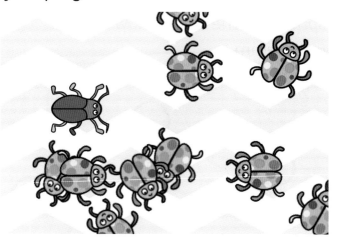

Part 1

Step	Instruction
❶	Start program when Green Flag is clicked
❷	Go to: x = 120 y = 0
❸	Point in direction −90
❹	Erase all pen drawings

Part 2

Step	Instruction
❶	Start program when this sprite is clicked
❷	Turn 60 degrees to the left
❸	Glide 1 second to random position
❹	Stamp with pen

Did you know?

- Games can be good for your body and mind. Players can develop quicker reactions and learn to do more than one thing at once.
- However, playing video games for too long is bad for your body and mind. It can prevent you from learning new things and stop you from playing outdoor games. This is very bad for your health.

 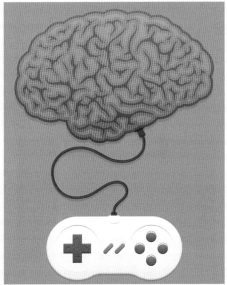

What can you do?

Read and review what you can do.

- ✔ I know about algorithms with a sub-routine.
- ✔ I can develop algorithms and programs with repetition.
- ✔ I can systematically test programs.

Great! Now you know sub-routines and can systematically test programs.

Control systems

Get started!

1 Do you remember some devices have computers inside them? Where can they be found?

2 List some examples that are in the home.

3 Discuss with your partner what the computer controls in these devices shown below:

In this unit, you will learn about inputs, outputs, control systems, types of software and some file types.

You will learn:
- about control systems
- about application and systems software
- about data recorded by input devices
- about information communicated by output devices
- that different types of files have different sizes.

Warm up

Work with a partner.

1 What is the difference between hardware and software?
2 State which of these objects shown below are hardware and which are software:

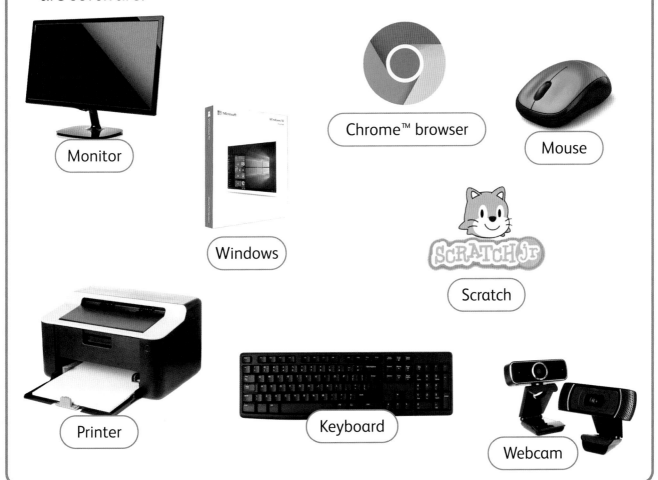

Monitor

Windows

Chrome™ browser

Mouse

Scratch

Printer

Keyboard

Webcam

Do you remember?

Before starting this unit, check that you:
- know the differences between hardware and software
- know about manual and automatic input devices
- know that there are different types of files
- know that computers control machines
- know about some common 'Internet of Things' devices.

Control systems
Where can they be found?

Many devices are operated using a control system.

The simplest form of a control system requires an input device to record data, a processor to process that data, and an output device that the processor instructs.

A microwave has a control system:

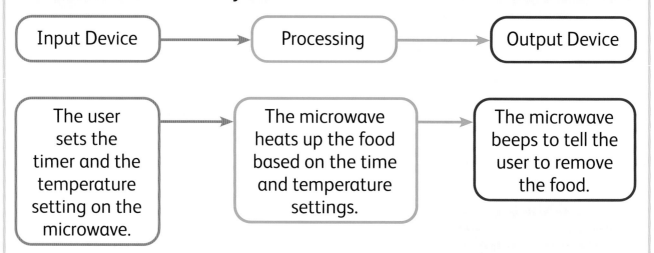

| Input Device | → | Processing | → | Output Device |

| The user sets the timer and the temperature setting on the microwave. | → | The microwave heats up the food based on the time and temperature settings. | → | The microwave beeps to tell the user to remove the food. |

In the home:
Control systems can be found in many modern appliances such as ovens, washing machines, refrigerators, automatic tea/coffee makers, microwaves and air conditioners. For example, in a clothes dryer:

| The user sets the drying time using a dial or keypad. | → | The processor uses the input data to send signals to the drum and heater. | → | The drum spins and the heater switches on, until the dryer stops and beeps. |

In the manufacturing industry:

Control systems can be found where processes need to be regulated.

For example, in a factory, if a can is being filled with soda to a certain level, computers are used to control this level.

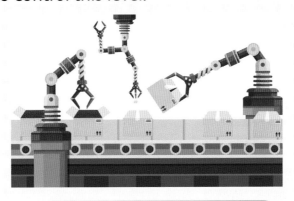

| A sensor checks how far the soda is from the top of the can. | → | A processor instructs the soda to be poured until the sensor data shows that the soda is at the top of the can. | → | The filling of the can stops. |

In robotics:

Control systems are used to control the movement of a robot. For example, a robot vacuum avoids collisions with obstacles while cleaning the floor.

| A distance sensor checks how close objects are. | → | The processor tells the wheels to keep moving until the input data suggests an object is close. | → | The wheels change direction so that the robot avoids the object. |

In vehicles:

A vehicle's cruise control system checks the distance to nearby vehicles and adjusts its speed and distance accordingly.

| A distance sensor senses how close other vehicles are. | → | The processor checks whether the input data is a safe distance from another vehicle. | → | The brakes are applied if another vehicle is too close. |

Practise

Discuss with your group.

1 Can you name three places where control systems can be found?

2 Can you name three devices in the home that contain control systems?

3 Which of the following probably does not have a computer control system?

   a Traffic lights

   b A security alarm

   c An air-conditioning unit

   d An outdoor pizza oven

4 With a partner, discuss the control system of a refrigerator. What are the inputs? What is processed? What are the outputs?

Application and system software

Computer programs are known as software. There are two types of software: application software and system software.

Application software are programs that carry out a specific task or solve a particular problem. For example:

- If you want to type a letter to your friend, you use word processing software.
- If you want to store data, you use database software.
- If you want to work with numbers, you use spreadsheet software.
- If you would like to draw a picture on the computer, you use drawing software.
- If you would like to surf the World Wide Web, you use web browser software.
- If you would like to listen to music, you use audio software.
- A computer game is also a type of application software.

System software are programs that control how the computer system functions. System software is used to:

Operating systems

- manage files and memory – it organises all files on your computer and how they are stored
- manage security – it repairs, backs up and provides virus protection to your computer
- manage the order of tasks when multiple programs are running at the same time
- control input and output devices such as printers, monitors and cameras.

Android™ platform

The operating system oversees many of these programs. The operating system is also part of the system software.

Chrome OS™ operating system

Keywords

application software: software programs that carry out a particular task or solve a particular problem

system software: software that manages the operations of the computer and its resources

operating system: a type of system software that manages programs and hardware

Practise

1 In groups, discuss which operating system you have on your computer, tablet or smartphone.

2 Match each operating system icon with its name.

| A | |
| B | |

| Chrome OS™ operating system |
| Android™ platform |

3 True or false?

   a Computer games are an example of application software.

   b A word processor is an example of system software.

   c An operating system is type of system software.

   d A program such as Scratch is a type of system software.

4 Which of these statements are **not** true?

   a An operating system manages files and memory.

   b An operating system manages the order of a computer's tasks.

   c An operating system can create a document such as a letter.

   d An operating system manages input and output devices.

Recorded data
Input devices

Learn

All computer systems, including control systems, input information or data from an input device. Different types of data are recorded by different input devices, depending on the application.

> Do you remember some of the common input devices for a desktop computer?

A mouse is an input device that uses a beam of light to track its position on a desk. As you move the mouse, the mouse pointer moves on the computer screen.

A keyboard is another common input device. As the keys on the keyboard are pressed, an electronic signal is sent to the computer that tells it what letter, number or symbol was pressed. The correct information is then displayed on the computer screen.

Control systems are attached to input devices called sensors. Sensors are special devices that detect changes in the environment such as:

- temperature
- light
- motion.

There are many other types of sensors that record many other types of data.

Temperature sensors are found in appliances such as refrigerators, rice cookers, microwaves, and air-conditioning units.

For example, in a rice cooker, the temperature of the rice is measured, and this temperature data is sent to the processor. It processes this information to decide whether to increase or decrease the heat in the cooker.

Light sensors can be found in streetlights. They detect the amount of light in the surrounding area.

The sensor sends data about the amount of light to the processor. It processes this data to decide whether to turn on the streetlight.

Infrared sensors are used in many remote-control systems. The remote control sends infrared light when a button is pressed.

The infrared sensor on a device such as a TV sends data about the amount of infrared light it receives to the processor. It processes this data to decide what to do – for example, to turn on the television.

A data logger is an electronic device that contains a sensor to sense data, a computer chip to process it and some way to store data. They are devices that are often left by themselves to gather data. The data and processed information are collected at a later date.

A weather station data logger can record and save information about the weather over a length of time.

It can record the wind speed, wind direction, temperature, and amount of rainfall.

Keyword

data logger: an electronic device that contains a sensor, a processor and some way to store data

Practise

1 Select the most appropriate sensor from the word bank below.

(distance) (light) (motion) (temperature) (infrared)

  a Which sensor is used to detect a car near a traffic light?

  b Which sensor is used to detect the signal from your car radio remote?

  c A light switches on when someone walks close to your home. Which type of sensor is being used?

  d Which sensor in an air-conditioning unit detects when it is too hot or cold. and adjusts its settings?

2 Discuss the following with a partner:

  a What is a sensor?

  b What is a data logger?

  c What is the difference between a sensor and a data logger?

  d Draw a diagram to represent the input, process and output of a motion security system.

Output data
Output devices

Learn

Computer systems are attached to output devices. Output devices take information that has been processed by the computer system and create a physical or visible action that a user can understand.

A **monitor** or **screen** is an output device. It allows you to see information from a computer, such as text, graphics and video.

A **printer** is an output device that lets you see text and graphics printed on paper.

Here are more examples of output devices.

Output	Device	Example
Light	Bulbs or lamps	Light output from motion sensor
Sound	Buzzers Speakers Bells	Sound output from smoke detector

Movement	Robotic arm Motors	The movement of a robotic arm is based on processed data from a proximity sensor
Data or information – text, graphics or video	Monitor Printer Displays	Car display monitor shows information about the car

Do you remember any other output devices that are often attached to a desktop computer?

Practise

1 Can you determine the **type of output** and the **output device** from the following control system examples?

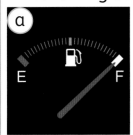   

2 Discuss with your group.
  a Describe three different types of outputs that you can get from control systems.
  b Which devices in the home use these types of outputs?

File sizes

Different types of files such as text, audio, images, videos and games have different sizes. They need different amounts of storage space on your computer.

Text files are made up of letters, numbers, symbols and blank spaces. Each character takes up a very small amount of storage.

Text files, such as a letter or report, take up the least amount of storage.

Audio files, such as a voice note or a song, take up more storage than a text file. A CD can store more than 100 songs of good quality audio.

Image files, such as high-quality photographs, take up a lot more storage space than a text file. They often need more storage space than one song.

A high-quality **video** or **movie** file needs more storage space than audio, text or image files.

Did you know?

Computer and video game files have a range of sizes. A game can occupy a small amount of storage or a large amount of storage. It depends on the quality of the images, animation and videos that are used in the game. Higher quality audio and video files also require more storage.

Keyword
voice note: a short audio file created by speaking

Practise

1 Is the storage space needed for 20 high quality photographs more or less than for two pages of a typed document? Give a reason for your answer.

2 You have recorded approximately 28 minutes of high-quality video of your birthday party. Would the storage space for the video be larger or smaller than for a voice note to your parents? Give a reason for your answer.

3 Which of the following usually requires the least amount of storage?

- A music song
- A photograph
- A movie video
- Text

4 Which of the following usually requires the most amount of storage?

- A music song
- A photograph
- A movie video
- Text

Go further

1 Discuss with your group.

a What do distance sensors do?

b Where can distance sensors be found?

c Can you list some other places where distance sensors might be useful?

2 What type of output can be produced if you have a distance sensor in your car?

3 Can a data logger be used to store the data produced by a distance sensor?

4
- A home security camera system records a video of a person once the person approaches the front door of the house.
- A bird watcher sets up a camera to take pictures of a bird's nest every hour for an entire week.

a Which one requires more storage: the home security camera system or the bird watcher's camera?

b What type of sensor could the bird watcher's camera use?

c What type of application software would you require to view these files?

Challenge yourself!

1 A smoke detector alarm goes off in your home.

   a What type of input data or information do you think the control system receives?

   b What type of output does the detector produce?

2 There are sensors that detect smoke, pressure, chemicals, rain, gas, colours, vibrations and many others. For each of these sensors listed, research what it is used for and where it can be found. Can you list any more sensors?

3 An operating system is required for most computer systems to work correctly. List all the different functions that an operating system performs. You may need to do some research.

4 A video doorbell is rung, and the camera captures a short video and voice message left by the guest. Which one takes up the most storage: the video or the voice message? Discuss with a partner.

My project

Work in groups of four.

1 You and your group have decided to create a smart-home model. Your smart home uses a number of control systems throughout the home.

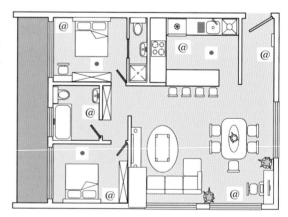

   • List four devices in your smart home that will utilise control systems.

   • State what input devices are used, and what data is recorded from these devices.

   • State what output devices are used and what sort of outputs they produce.

   • Draw a layout of your house showing where the devices may be located.

Key:
• smoke   @ light

Hint: You can use a key to indicate where the sensors are located in your drawing.

2 Jack's security camera in his home captures ten separate 5-minute videos of delivery companies dropping off packages. He also has ten songs that he likes to listen to on his computer. Which files are likely to be larger – the video footage or the songs? Explain your answer.

3 Viti's dad bought her a laptop. When she started up her laptop, she saw the following icons:

a Tell Viti what software she has on her laptop.

b Explain to her the difference between the two main types of software and what they are used for.

What can you do?

Read and review what you can do.

✔ I know where a control system is used.

✔ I know the difference between application and systems software.

✔ I know about some types of data recorded by input devices.

✔ I know about some information communicated by output devices.

✔ I know that different types of files have different sizes.

Great effort! Now you know about control systems, sensors, output devices and file sizes!

Drawing shapes

Get started!

Work in groups of four. Discuss what shapes you see in each picture below.

Picture 1

Picture 2

In this unit, you will display shapes with MakeCode for micro:bit.

You will learn:

- to develop algorithms with different outputs from different inputs
- to develop programs to produce outputs from inputs
- to develop programs using count-controlled and forever loops.

Warm up

Work in pairs. The shapes below follow a pattern.
What is the next shape in each sequence?

1

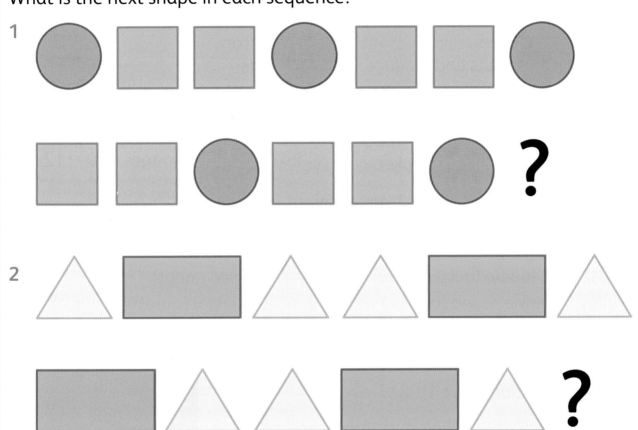

2

Do you remember?

Before starting this unit, check that you:
- can follow, understand and edit algorithms with repetition
- can test different parts of a program
- know about count-controlled and forever loops.

In this unit, you will use the micro:bit. There is an online chapter all about MakeCode for micro:bit.

Using physical computing devices
Understanding inputs and outputs

Learn

The micro:bit is a physical computing device. It can accept several inputs and produce several outputs.

Some inputs are the **buttons**, the **microphone**, and **sensors** such as **light**, **touch** and **temperature** sensors.

Some of the outputs are the **LEDs** and **sound** through a built-in speaker.

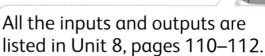
All the inputs and outputs are listed in Unit 8, pages 110–112.

Producing different outputs from different inputs

We can program the micro:bit to produce different outputs based on different inputs. For example, we can make the micro:bit:

- display a square (output) when Button A is pressed (input)
- play a twinkle sound (output) when the touch sensor is pressed (input).

Before creating the code, we must first write the algorithm.

Output for the first input:

Step	Instruction (Part 1)
①	Start program when Button A is pressed
②	Show square on LED display

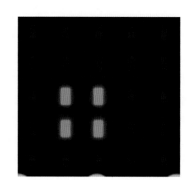

When Button A is pressed, four LEDs light up. They form a square shape on the micro:bit's LED display.

Output for the second input:

Step	Instruction (Part 2)
①	Start program when the logo is touched
②	Play twinkle sound until done

The touch sensor on the micro:bit is located on the logo at the top middle of the micro:bit.

When the touch sensor is pressed, the micro:bit will play a twinkle sound.

The micro:bit will produce one of these two outputs based on which input it receives.

> **Keywords**
> **physical computing device:** a device that interacts with the world around it
> **input:** sends information into the device
> **output:** sends information out of the device
> **touch sensor:** a sensor that can tell if the device is touched in that area

Practise

1 Write an algorithm for the micro:bit, as follows:
   - When the logo is touched, it should play a giggle sound.
   - When Button A is pressed, it should display a square 3 LEDs wide and 3 LEDs high anywhere on the micro:bit display.
   - When Button B is pressed, it should show a heart icon.

Part 1

Step	Instruction
1	Start program when ___
2	Play ___

Part 2

Step	Instruction
1	Start program when ___
2	Show ...

Part 3

Step	Instruction
1	Start program when ___
2	Show ___

2 Add the following to the algorithm in question **1** so that:
   - when Buttons A and B are pressed together, the micro:bit should display two icons; a **Yes** icon then a **No** icon
   - The two icons should be displayed for 1 second each and this sequence should be repeated twice.

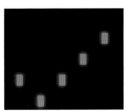 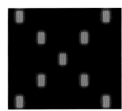

Programming the micro:bit

Learn

We can create the code for the algorithm on page 170 that produces different outputs from different inputs, as shown below.

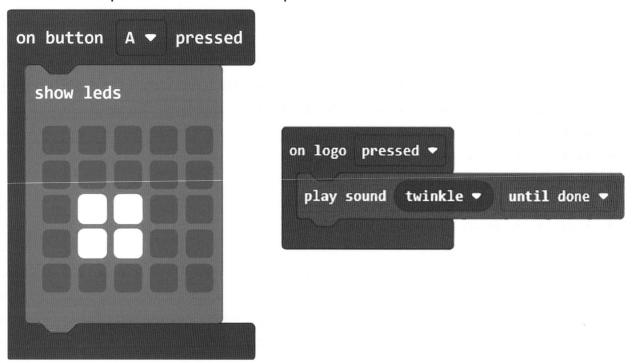

Follow these steps to create this program using MakeCode for micro:bit:

1 Open a new project.
2 Delete the **on start** and **forever** blocks from the programming area.
3 Add the blocks of code shown above.
4 Click the **Play** button on the left of the screen to start the simulator.
5 Press **Button A** and touch the logo to run the program. Debug any errors.

 If using the physical device, you should follow the additional instructions on using the physical micro:bit for running a program.

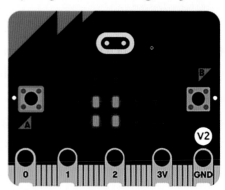

Practise

1 If you haven't done so already, create the program on the previous page in MakeCode for micro:bit.

2 Change your program so the micro:bit displays the square on the LED display when **Button B** is pressed instead.

3 Add code to match the algorithm below. In this algorithm, the micro:bit displays a triangle for two seconds and then a square when it is shaken.

Step	Instruction (Part 1)
1	Start program when the micro:bit is shaken
2	Show triangle on LED display
3	Pause for 2 seconds (2000 ms)
4	Show square on LED display

We can display a triangle and square on the micro:bit by lighting the LEDs as shown.

4 Click **Play** and test your program.

5 Check if you get the desired results. Does the program match the algorithm?

6 Add code to match the algorithm below. The micro:bit will show an arrow pointing north (up direction) when **Button A** is pressed.

Step	Instruction
1	When the program is started
2	Set marker down

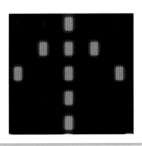

7 Click **Play** and test your program.

8 Check if you get the desired results. Does the program match the algorithm?

9 Test your program in parts to find and debug any errors.

Count-controlled and indefinite (forever) loops

Learn

As previously stated, there are three types of loops:

- Indefinite (forever) loops
- Count-controlled loops
- Condition-controlled loops.

We can use these loops to control the micro:bit. While the blocks that are used in MakeCode for micro:bit are different to those in Scratch, the end result is the same.

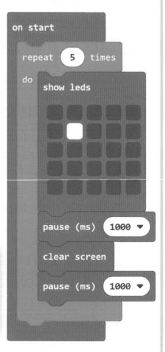

Program micro:bit using a count-controlled loop

On the MakeCode for micro:bit app, we can use the **repeat do** block to create a count-controlled loop.

Remember, if we want to run some code five times, a count-controlled loop will count the number of iterations and repeat the instructions inside the loop five times.

In this example, the micro:bit will run five iterations when the program is started.

The micro:bit will light an LED for 1 second and then turn it off for 1 second. This repeats five times. You should recall that 1000 ms is 1 second.

Program using an indefinite (forever) loop

On MakeCode for micro:bit, we can use the **Forever** block to represent a forever loop. It will repeat instructions inside the loop over and over without ever stopping.

In this example, the micro:bit will display a south arrow (down direction) for 1 second on the LED display and clear the screen for 1 second. This repeats forever.

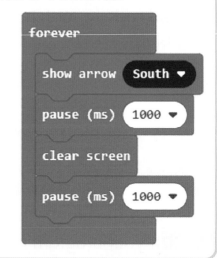

Practise

Create two programs using MakeCode for micro:bit, as follows:

1 Open a new project.

2 Create the code to flash one LED on for 1 second, and then turn it off for one second. You can use the first part of the **Learn** panel to help you.

3 Add code to flash the south arrow on for 1 second and then off for 1 second. You can use the second part of the **Learn** panel to help you.

4 Now add in a loop so that the LED and then the south arrow flash on and off in sequence four times in total.

5 Run and test your program. Does it work as expected? If not, make corrections and test again.

6 Now you need to amend your program so that the LED and then the south arrow flash on and off in sequence forever.

7 Test your program and correct any errors.

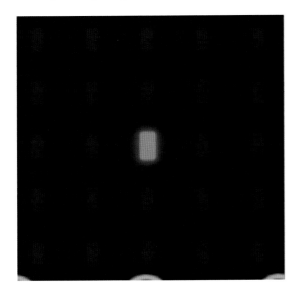
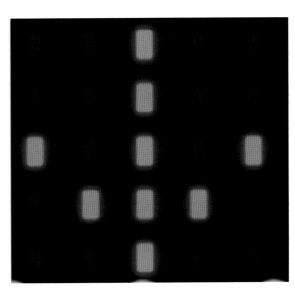

Follow the additional instructions if using the physical micro:bit when running a program.

Go further

Computational thinking

Write the algorithm for the micro:bit to display a rectangle on the LED display when the program is started.

1 Open a new project.
2 Create the program for the algorithm you wrote above.
3 Click the **Play** button to run the program. Check your results.
4 Add code to match the algorithms in the tables below. The algorithms instruct the micro:bit to:

- blink a curve four times when both **Buttons A** and **B** are pressed
- play two sounds twice when the program is started.

Part 1

Step	Instruction
1	Start program when Button A+B are pressed
2	Show LEDs for a curve (i.e. 5 LEDs)
3	Pause for 1 second (1000 ms)
4	Clear screen
5	Pause for 1 second (1000 ms)
6	Repeat steps 2 to 5 three more times

Part 2

Step	Instruction
1	Start program when the logo is touched
2	Play happy sound until done
3	Pause for 2 seconds (2000 ms)
4	Play sad sound until done
5	Pause for 2 seconds (2000 ms)
6	Repeat steps 2 to 5 one more time

You can use the **Show LEDs** block to make a curve.

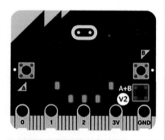

Test your programs in parts to find and debug any errors.

Challenge yourself!

1 Create a program for an algorithm for the micro:bit to display a sequence of letters, images and numbers as described below.

Step	Instruction
1	Start program when the micro:bit is shaken
2	Show letters "Hi" (i.e. 15 LEDs)
3	Pause for 1 second (1000 ms)
4	Clear screen
5	Play hello sound until done
6	Pause for 1 second (1000 ms)
7	Show a chess board icon
8	Pause for 1 second (1000 ms)
9	Clear screen
10	Play hello sound until done
11	Pause for 1 second (1000 ms)
12	Show string "5"
13	Pause for 1 second (1000 ms)
14	Clear screen
15	Play hello sound until done
16	Pause for 1 second (1000 ms)
17	Repeat steps 2 to 16 one more time

What are the three possible coding blocks that can be used to display letters and/or images on the micro:bit's LED display?

2 Click the **Play** button to test your program.

3 Check that you get the correct results.

4 Find and debug any errors.

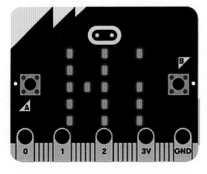 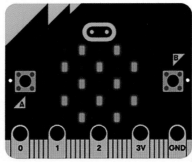 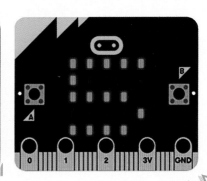

My project

1 Write an algorithm to do the following:

   - Display a diamond shape on the micro:bit's LED display when **Button A** is pressed.
   - Play a birthday melody to repeat once when **Button B** is pressed.

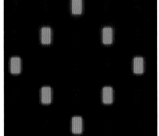

Part 1		Part 2	

2 Open a new project using MakeCode for micro:bit.

3 Create the program for the algorithm in Part 1.

4 Develop an algorithm for the micro:bit to display the letter 'N' and blink three times when the touch sensor (logo) is touched.

Step	Instruction
❶	Start program when logo is touched
❷	Show _____
❸	Pause _____
❹	Clear _____
❺	Pause _____
❻	Repeat _____

5 Write this algorithm as a program in MakeCode for micro:bit.

6 Develop a program to match the algorithm below for the micro:bit to show the east arrow and clear the screen repeatedly forever.

Step	Instruction
❶	Start program when Play button is pressed
❷	Show east arrow on LED display
❸	Pause for 1 second (1000 ms)
❹	Clear screen
❺	Pause for 1 second (1000 ms)
❻	Repeat steps 2 to 5 forever

Test and debug all your code.

Did you know?

We can program other physical computing devices, such as human-like robots that can talk.

- Sophia is a human-like robot that was first activated in February 2016.
- Cameras in Sophia's eyes are input devices which, when combined with computer programs, allow her to 'see'.
- She can follow faces, process speech and have conversations.
- Just like the micro:bit, Sophia can produce different outputs from different inputs.

What can you do?

Read and review what you can do.

- ✔ I can develop algorithms to produce different outputs from different inputs.
- ✔ I can develop programs to produce an output from an input.
- ✔ I can develop programs using count-controlled and forever loops.

Good job! Now you can program a physical computing device!

Glossary

A

application software: software programs that carry out a particular task or solve a particular problem

B

browser: a computer program for displaying and moving between web pages

C

ciphertext: encrypted data

client: a computer that connects to and uses the resources of a server

comment: a note explaining the meaning of a program's code

computer scientist: a person who uses computational thinking skills to work with computer hardware and software

condition-controlled loop: blocks of code are repeated until a condition is met

count-controlled loop: a type of loop where instructions are repeated a set number of times

counter: keeps track of the number of times a loop has run

cybercrime: criminal activities carried out by means of computers or the internet

D

data type: the values a field can store

database: an organised collection of related data

data logger: an electronic device that contains a sensor, a processor and some way to store data

debugging: finding and removing errors from a program

decomposition: a process used to break a task into simpler parts

decrypt: to convert a code into a form that can be read

drone: a remote-controlled, unmanned or pilotless aircraft

E

encryption: disguises data so that only people with access to a secret key can understand it

ethernet: another name for the copper cables used in wired networks

F

Forever block: repeats the code inside it over and over until you stop the program

forever loop: instructions that repeat over and over without stopping

format: the way in which something is arranged

H

hyperlink: a link from one web page to another

I

information: processed data

input: sends information into the device

input device: a piece of hardware that sends data to the micro:bit

instant messaging: a service where users can communicate in real time

internet: a worldwide network of computers and devices

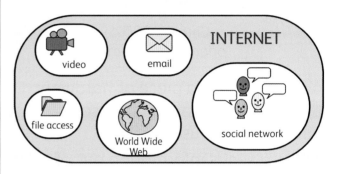

iteration: a single pass through a set of instructions

L

LED: a small light on the micro:bit.

N

network failure: when a network stops working properly due to hardware or software faults

NETWORK FAILURE

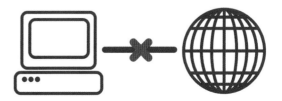

O

operating system: a type of system software that manages programs and hardware

Android™ platform

Chrome OS™ operating system

output device: a piece of hardware that allows the micro:bit to send information to us

output: sends information out of the device

P

physical computing device: a device that interacts with the world around it

plain text: refers to data before it is encrypted

plain text   Encrypted Email   plain text

R

radio wave: a way of sending information through the air

random: does not follow a pattern

raw data: not processed

Repeat block: Scratch code used for count-controlled loops

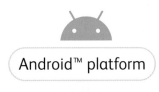

repetition: code that is run a number of times within a program

S

search: to look for

sensor: a device that detects an input from the environment, such as heat, light, sound or movement

server: a computer that provides services to other computers on a network

sub-routine: a set of instructions designed to perform a frequently-used operation

system software: software that manages the operations of the computer and its resources

systematically: testing in turn until we find the error

T

touch sensor: a sensor that can tell if the device is touched in that area

V

voice note: a short audio file created by speaking

W

website: a collection of linked web pages

Wi-Fi: a set of rules for devices communicating over wireless networks

wired: connecting devices in a network with physical wires

wireless: a way of connecting devices in a network via radio waves

World Wide Web: a large collection of linked web pages accessed by a browser

Acknowledgements

The Publishers would like to thank the following for permission to reproduce copyright material. Every effort has been made to trace or contact all copyright holders, but if any have been inadvertently overlooked, the Publishers will be pleased to make the necessary arrangements at the first opportunity.

Text acknowledgements
pp. 4, 40, 105, 114–115, 117, 119–122, 153, 168–169, 172–176, 178 © Used with permission from Microsoft; **pp. 4, 40–41, 153** © Chrome™ browser is a trademark of Google LLC. Google and Google Docs are trademarks of Google LLC and this book is not endorsed by or affiliated with Google in any way; **pp. 4, 6, 8–9, 12–18, 49, 55–59, 61, 74–77, 80–83, 85–89, 138–140, 142–150, 153, 158, 167, 174, 182** © Scratch is developed by the Lifelong Kindergarten Group at the MIT Media Lab. See http://scratch.mit.edu. Licensed under a Creative Commons Attribution-ShareAlike 2.0 Generic license (CC BY-SA 2.0); **pp. 40, 45** © Firefox is a trademark of the Mozilla Foundation in the U.S. and other countries.; **pp. 104–106, 108, 110–114, 116–118, 120–122, 168–179, 181** © Copyright Micro:bit Educational Foundation or Foundation partners; **pp. 176–158, 182** © Android™ platform is a trademark of Google LLC. Google and Google Docs are trademarks of Google LLC and this book is not endorsed by or affiliated with Google in any way; **pp. 157–158, 182** © Chrome OS™ operating system is a trademark of Google LLC. Google and Google Docs are trademarks of Google LLC and this book is not endorsed by or affiliated with Google in any way.

Photo acknowledgements
p. 4 *cc*, **p. 138** *cl* © Macro Vector/Adobe Stock Photo; **p. 4** *cr*, **p. 138** *cr* © Hadeev/Adobe Stock Photo; **p. 4** *cl*, **p. 153** *cl* © Tech Stock Studio/Adobe Stock Photo; **pp. 4**, **p. 29–30**, **p. 33**, **p. 40**, **pp. 99–100**, **pp. 114 –117**, **p. 120**, **p. 122**, **p. 153**, **p. 157**, **p. 167**, **p. 172**, **p. 174**, **p. 176**, **p. 180** © Used with permission from Microsoft; **p. 4** *cc*, **p. 40** *cc*, **p. 153** *cc* © Chrome™ browser is a trademark of Google LLC. Google and Google Docs are trademarks of Google LLC and this book is not endorsed by or affiliated with Google in any way; **p. 4** *cc*, **p. 153** *cr*, **p. 159** *cc* © Billion Photos.com/Adobe Stock Photo; **p. 4** *cl*, **p. 153** *cl* © Sergey Peterman/Adobe Stock Photo; **p. 4**, **p. 5–7**, **p. 12–18**, **p. 55–57**, **p. 80–87**, **p. 140–150**, **p. 153**, **p. 167**, **p. 181–182** © Scratch is developed by the Lifelong Kindergarten Group at the MIT Media Lab. See http://scratch.mit.edu. Licensed under a Creative Commons Attribution-ShareAlike 2.0 Generic license (CC BY-SA 2.0); **p. 4** *cc*, **p. 153** *cc*, **p. 159** *cc* © Gresei/Adobe Stock Photo; **p. 4** *cc*, **p. 153** *cr* © Dan 74/Adobe Stock Photo; **p. 5** *cc*, **p. 70** *cl* © Metamorworks/Adobe Stock Photo; **p. 5** *cr*, **p. 70** *cr* © Sompong Tom/Adobe Stock Photo; **p. 5** *cc*, **p. 70** *cl* © Sergey Ryzhov/Adobe Stock Photo; **p. 5** *cr*, **p. 70** *cr* © Es sarawuth/Adobe Stock Photo; **p. 5** *cc*, **p. 70** *cl* © Es sarawuth/Adobe Stock Photo; **p. 5** *cr*, **p. 70** *cr* © Es sarawuth/Adobe Stock Photo; **p. 6** *bl*, **p. 101** *bc* © Wanchai/Adobe Stock Photo; **p. 7** *cr*, **p. 68** *cc* © Miro Kovacevic/Adobe Stock Photo; **p. 20** © Dragon Images/Adobe Stock Photo; **p. 20** *cr* © Mnirat/Adobe Stock Photo; **p. 21** *cl* © Tang 90246/Adobe Stock Photo; **p. 21** *cr* © Destina/Adobe Stock Photo; **p. 22** *cc* © Vladimir Liverts/Adobe Stock Photo; **p. 22** *cr* © Michak Lootwijk/Adobe Stock Photo; **p. 22** *cc* © Fotomatrix/Adobe Stock Photo; **p. 22** *cr* © I 9370/Adobe Stock Photo; **p. 22** *cc* © Gamjai/Adobe Stock Photo; **p. 22** *cr* © Karen Roach/Adobe Stock Photo; **p. 22** *bl* © Phonlamai/Adobe Stock Photo; **p. 23** *cl* © Billion Photos.com/Adobe Stock Photo; **p. 23** *cr* © Tsung-Lin Wu/Adobe Stock Photo; **p. 25** *tr* © Magnetic MCC/Adobe Stock Photo; **p. 25** *br* © Andrey Popov/Adobe Stock Photo; **p. 26** *cr* © Paltu/Adobe Stock Photo; **p. 27** *tr* © Pixel-Shot/Adobe Stock Photo; **p. 28** © Paper Owl/Adobe Stock Photo; **p. 34** *tr* © Bobboz/Adobe Stock Photo; **p. 35** *tr* © Vibe Images/Adobe Stock Photo; **p. 36** © Alphaspirit/Adobe Stock Photo; **p. 40** *cr* © The Firefox logo is a trademark of the Mozilla Foundation in the U.S. and other countries; **p. 42** *tr* © Anton/Adobe Stock Photo; **p. 42** *br* © Natchapon/Adobe Stock Photo; **p. 43** *tl* © Tetiana/Adobe Stock Photo; **p. 43** *cl* © Fotolia Design 20/Adobe Stock Photo; **p. 43** *cl* © Farbai/Adobe Stock Photo; **p. 48** © Olha Tsiplyar/Adobe Stock Photo; **p. 49** *cl*, *cl* © Hasmik/Adobe Stock Photo; **p. 49** *cr* © Hasmik/Adobe Stock Photo; **p. 50** *cr* © Viesturs/Adobe Stock Photo; **p. 52** *cr* © Vicgmyr/Adobe Stock Photo; **p. 53** *br* © Cary Blade/Adobe Stock Photo; **p. 59** *bl* © Di Anna/Adobe Stock Photo; **p. 59** *bc* © Di Anna/Adobe Stock Photo; **p. 59** *bc* © Di Anna/Adobe Stock Photo; **p. 59** *br* © Di Anna/Adobe Stock Photo; **p. 62** *cl* © Chas 53/Adobe Stock Photo; **p. 62** *cr* © Marcelo Trad Nery/Adobe Stock Photo; **p. 62** *cl*, **p. 152** *cl* © Nosoroqua/Adobe Stock Photo; **p. 62** *cr* © Fizkes/Adobe Stock Photo; **p. 66** *cc* © Golubovy/Adobe Stock Photo; **p. 67** *br* © Gorodenkoff/Adobe Stock Photo; **p. 68** *cc* © ES Sarawuth/Adobe Stock Photo; **p. 68** *cr* © ES Sarawuth/Adobe Stock Photo; **p. 68** *cr* © Metamor Works/Adobe Stock Photo; **p. 68** *cr* © Leonid Andronov/Adobe Stock Photo; **p. 69** *tc* © Zapp 2 Photo/Adobe Stock Photo; **p. 69** *tr* © Itsanan/Adobe Stock Photo; **p. 69** © Monopoly 919/Adobe Stock Photo; **p. 69** *cr* © Yurakrasil/Adobe Stock Photo; **p. 69** *br* © Reuters/Alamy Stock Photo; **p. 71** *cl* © Chesky/Adobe Stock Photo; **p. 71** *cr* © Pressmaster/Adobe Stock Photo; **p. 71** *cl* © Damian/Adobe Stock Photo; **p. 71** *cr* © Etemwanich/Adobe Stock Photo; **p. 71** *cl* © Reuters/Alamy Stock Photo; **p. 71** *cr* © Zapp 2 Photo/Adobe Stock Photo; **p. 89** *cr* © Pixel-Shot/Adobe Stock Photo; **p. 90** *cr* © Digital Genetics/Adobe Stock Photo; **p. 92** *br* © JYPIX/Adobe Stock Photo; **p. 93** *bf* © Sheilaf 2002/Adobe Stock Photo; **p. 94** *br* © Madedee/Adobe Stock Photo; **p. 95** *bc* © Billion Photos.com/Adobe Stock Photo; **p. 96** *br* © Luis Louro/Adobe Stock Photo; **p. 97** *cr* © Drobot Dean/Adobe Stock Photo; **p. 100** *br* © Zephyr P/Adobe Stock Photo; **p. 103** *cc* © Mikhail/Adobe Stock Photo; **p. 104** *cl* © InsideCreativeHouse/Adobe Stock Photo; **p. 103** *cc* © Pixel Shot/Adobe Stock Photo; **p. 104** *cr* © Junce 11/Adobe Stock Photo; **p. 104** *cc* © Zilvergolf/Adobe Stock Photo; **p. 104** *cc* © Pixel Shot/Adobe Stock Photo; **p. 106**, **p. 108**, **pp. 112–114**, **p. 116**, **pp. 170–173**, **pp. 175–178** © Copyright Micro:bit Educational Foundation or Foundation partners; **p. 122** *cr* © Shanvood/Adobe Stock Photo; **p. 123** *cr*, **p. 136** *cc* © Hachette UK; **p. 125** *cc*, **p. 181** © Rawpixel.com/Adobe Stock Photo; **p. 125** *cr* © Rawpixel.com/Adobe Stock Photo; **p. 125** *br* © Yaroslav/Adobe Stock Photo; **p. 126** *tr* © Sudok 1/Adobe Stock Photo; **p. 126** *cl* © Press Master/Adobe Stock Photo; **p. 126** *cr* © Billion Photos.com/Adobe Stock Photo; **p. 127** *bc* © Ty/Adobe Stock Photo; **p. 129** *tr* © Nicescene/Adobe Stock Photo; **p. 129** *cr* © Tashatuvango/Adobe Stock Photo; **p. 129** *cr*, **p. 180** *tr* © Frank Peters/Adobe Stock Photo; **p. 134** *bl* © Kichigin 19/Adobe Stock Photo; **p. 134** *br* © Aram/Adobe Stock Photo; **p. 141** *tr* © Lasha Kilasonia/Adobe Stock Photo; **p. 151** *cl* © Redpixel/Adobe Stock Photo; **p. 151** *cr* © Brain with computer game pad/Adobe Stock Photo; **p. 152** *cc* © Sergiy 1975/Adobe Stock Photo; **p. 152** © Ekostsov/Adobe Stock Photo; **p. 155** *tc* © Alfmaler/Shutterstock.com; **p. 155** *bc* © Lightfield Studios/Adobe Stock Photo; **p. 156** *cc* © Temp 64 GTX/Adobe Stock Photo; **p. 157** *cr*, **p. 180** *cc* Mojang © 2009-2022. "Minecraft" is a trademark of Mojang AB; **p. 157** *cr*, *cl*, **p. 157** *cc* © The Android robot is reproduced or modified from work created and shared by Google and used according to terms described in the Creative Commons 3.0 Attribution License; **p. 157** *br*, **p. 158** *cl*, **p. 182** *cc* © Chrome OS™ operating system is a trademark of Google LLC. Google and Google Docs are trademarks of Google LLC and this book is not endorsed by or affiliated with Google in any way; **p. 160** *tr* © BNP Design Studio/Adobe Stock Photo; **p. 160** *cc* © Viperagp/Adobe Stock Photo; **p. 161** *tr*, **p. 180** *br* © Ake/Adobe Stock Photo; **p. 162** *cr*, **p. 182** *cc* © Hervé Rouveure/Adobe Stock Photo; **p. 162** *br* © Nikky Tok/Adobe Stock Photo; **p. 163** *tr* © Phonlamaiphoto/Adobe Stock Photo; **p. 163** *cr* © Now Design/Shutterstock.com; **p. 163** *bl* © Ytemha 34/Adobe Stock Photo; **p. 163** *bc* © Bubutu/Adobe Stock Photo; **p. 163** *bc* © Metamor Works/Adobe Stock Photo; **p. 163** *br* © Think B/Adobe Stock Photo; **p. 164** *tr* © Kaspars Grinvalds/Adobe Stock Photo; **p. 164** *cr* © Antonio Francois/Adobe Stock Photo; **p. 164** *cr* © Rishav/Adobe Stock Photo; **p. 164** *cr* © Guru XOX/Adobe Stock Photo; **p. 167** *cc* © Google Classroom is a trademark of Google LLC. Google and Google Docs are trademarks of Google LLC and this book is not endorsed by or affiliated with Google in any way; **p. 168** *cl* © Raul H/Adobe Stock Photo; **p. 168** *cr* © 3000 ad/Adobe Stock Photo; **p. 179** *tr* © Nur Photo/Contributor/Getty Images; **p. 180** *cr* © Mnirat/Adobe Stock Photo.

t = top, *b* = bottom, *l* = left, *r* = right, *c* = centre